Estate Planning--
After the 1976
Tax Reform Act

Estate Planning--
After the 1976
Tax Reform Act

Edward E. Milam
D. Larry Crumbley

amacom

**A Division of
American Management Associations**

Certain portions of this book appeared in *Handbook of Wealth Management* by Leo Barnes and Stephan Feldman. © 1977 by McGraw-Hill Book Company. Used with permission.

Library of Congress Cataloging in Publication Data

Milam, Edward E.
   Estate planning, after the 1976 Tax reform act.

   Includes index.
     1. Inheritance and transfer tax--United States.
   2. Gifts--Taxation--United States. 3. Estate planning
   --United States. I. Crumbley, D. Larry, joint author.
   II. Title.
   KF6572.M5   343'.73'053   78-970
   ISBN 0-8144-5468-2

First Printing

Preface

THE Tax Reform Act of 1976 has caused sweeping changes in the estate and gift areas. In fact, these changes have been so dramatic, and so extensive, that they are surpassed in scope only by the original estate and gift tax legislation.

Estate planning is still possible. Since the estate tax was removed from approximately two-thirds of the current estates, the tax burden has shifted to the large estates. For example, the new rates reach the top rate of 70 percent at $5 million; whereas the *old* estate tax rates reached a maximum of 77 percent for a taxable estate of more than $10 million. Thus, estate planning is quite critical for large estates if they are to avoid the erosion of estate assets by federal and state death taxes.

Even though the tax changes have been far-reaching, the effect on any particular taxpayer depends entirely on his own specific circumstances.

To be in the best possible position, taxpayers should first be aware of all the property they own and, secondly, resolve in their minds how the property might best be distributed among future heirs. As soon as these steps are taken, expert estate and gift planning advice should be sought in order to ensure that these wishes are fulfilled at the minimum tax cost.

The major areas to scrutinize are explained in this volume. One of the most pervasive provisions of the Reform Act is that dealing with the adjusted carry-over tax basis for property passing to an heir. The effect of this rule will become more apparent as time progresses. Particular attention must be given each year to the difference between the market value and the adjusted carry-over basis of all property, especially in light of the prospective heirs' income tax status. Another major provision to be wary of is the generation-skipping tax when reviewing wills for changes prompted by the Reform Act. Careful analysis will avoid unexpected hardship years after an estate has been probated.

All taxpayers and their estate planners must be aware of the ramifications of the Reform Act, not only currently, but also for several years to come. As is usually the case with new tax legislation, many provisions will be defined and refined further through future regulations and court decisions, which will restrict, modify, and expand many of the new rules.

Edward E. Milam
D. Larry Crumbley

Contents

1

The Estate-Planning Process

Estate planning is social work among the rich.
Robert Brosterman

ANYONE with income or property must be concerned with estate planning. It may even be more important to the owner of a medium-size estate than a large estate, because the waste of a single asset in such an estate could prevent the accomplishment of objectives and bring hardship to the family. In other words, everyone who owns assets needs an estate plan. The estate plan might be reflected by a simple will or by a complex arrangement consisting of several of the estate-planning devices or tools available

1

to the estate owner. The massive changes in the estate tax area by the Tax Reform Act of 1976 make it imperative that all taxpayers review their current estate plan.

Because there are differences in peoples' objectives, attitudes, temperaments, and net assets, the estate plan of an individual should be designed to meet his specific needs and satisfy his specific objectives. Moreover, each plan must reflect the responsibilities of the person for whom it is drawn. Estate planning is different in details for every individual, but the process is basically the same for everyone. It can be broken conveniently into five steps:

1. Gathering the facts.
2. Evaluating the obstacles of estate impairment.
3. Designing the plan.
4. Implementing the plan.
5. Reviewing the plan.

GATHERING THE FACTS

The facts themselves serve as the basis for all other procedures. Obtaining the facts may seem to be a simple task, but in many cases it is the most challenging part of the estate-planning process. The facts needed can be classified into four categories: (1) domicile, (2) property, (3) beneficiaries, and (4) the individual's objectives.

Domicile

Domicile is important because it determines the law that will govern the validity of the will and its provisions. Domicile determines how title to property is held: community property versus separate property, and joint tenancy versus a tenancy in common. Because the differences that exist between real property laws of differing states are significant, the domicile of the estate owner must be determined before plans are formulated.

Property

A complete inventory of a taxpayer's assets and liabilities should be gathered. Use of the schedules prepared by Arthur Young & Co., which are reprinted as an appendix, can be quite helpful. Detailed information should be obtained with regard to all business and personal assets and liabilities. Such data would include insurance policies, powers of appointment, property owned separately and jointly, business interests, retirement and death benefits, claims under wills and trusts, and rights in future interests. In addition to these data, full information about the estate owner's obligations must be secured. These details include information about personal debts, business debts, accrued taxes, mortgages, leases, installment contracts, and all other debts, including contingent liabilities.

Special problems concerning an estate owner's business interests often arise in the analysis of his property, especially when they amount to a large portion of his estate. These business interests may be held in the form of sole proprietorships, partnerships, stock in a closely held corporation or Subchapter S corporation,* or any combination of these.

---

* A corporation's stockholders may elect to be a Subchapter S corporation which allows the corporation to avoid the corporate tax.

Business ownership causes a problem of valuation. These interests must be properly valued for estate tax purposes in accordance with the Internal Revenue Code and Regulations. Another problem is the determination and the ability of the business to produce income for the benefit of the taxpayer's heirs after his death or retirement. Even though the business is the chief source of a taxpayer's income and wealth, and will continue to be as long as he actively manages its affairs, it may not continue to be profitable in his absence or after his death. Upon the death of the taxpayer, the business interest becomes an investment of an estate, and it is valuable only if it continues to be profitable. Thus, care must be used in an evaluation of a person's business interests.

Beneficiaries

Facts concerning the beneficiaries of the estate owner must be gathered and accumulated by the estate owner or his estate-planning team.* These facts should include the names and birthdates of the estate owner and all of his beneficiaries. An evaluation should be made of the estate owner's responsibility to his family. Such personal information as the character of the estate owner's spouse and other heirs and their business abilities should be considered. A taxpayer's state of health, the wealth now available to his heirs, their financial needs, and the attitudes of individual beneficiaries toward each

* An estate-planning team is often composed of an attorney, a certified public accountant (CPA), a trust officer, and a life insurance underwriter. This estate-planning team can help in the selection of an executor or executrix.

other are important. In summary, an estate owner should obtain data about the health, wealth, education, character, and living needs of all his beneficiaries.[1]

Objectives

Finally, the objectives of the estate owner—his attitude and intentions toward the financial maintenance and security of his family—must be formulated. Many people feel that their heirs should have complete and unrestricted freedom to use the assets left to them, while others have a fear of entrusting substantial amounts of money in lump sums to their beneficiaries. Making such a determination, which is critical in the development of an estate plan, is very often the most difficult phase of gathering the facts.

In addition to gathering the facts, an estate owner must determine and evaluate his existing estate plan. Whether the estate owner is aware of it or not, he has an estate plan that may have been developed consciously or accidentally. Therefore, a taxpayer must accumulate information concerning all gifts, trusts, wills, and reversionary interests created or possessed by himself.[2]

This task of gathering the facts may appear to be tedious and dull, but it is often the most challenging and important part of the estate-planning process. Many estate owners who have not made such a thorough analysis of their estates have been surprised at the results. Such an analysis is necessary to lay a firm foundation for the remainder of the estate-planning process.

EVALUATING THE OBSTACLES OF ESTATE IMPAIRMENT

The second phase of the estate-planning process is an evaluation of the obstacles that could impair the value of the estate. An estate owner and the members of his estate-planning team must be aware of the many forces that can shrink the value of his estate and deny him the attainment of his objectives. Some of the more obvious of these impairments are the cost of the last illness, funeral expenses, estate administration expenses, and federal estate tax. Consideration must be given to all debts of great magnitude and long duration, such as mortgages, installment contracts, and business obligations. Attention must also be directed toward unpaid income and property taxes as well as state inheritance taxes. These are just a few of the more obvious obstacles.

According to Pfeffer, there are four classes of risk encountered in estate conservation problems. These risks are business, investment, legal, and tax risks.[3]

Business Risks

The management of any business is subject to a wide spectrum of risks, and competent managerial personnel must have the ability to successfully operate the firm. Some relevant questions for estate planning are (1) whether or not the management has the technical ability and training to continue profitable operation of the firm; (2) whether or not there are any heirs or key employees who have the aptitude, temperament, and capacity to be potential successors to the management; and (3) whether or not additional capital contributions will be necessary to maintain the current level of earnings.[4] Moreover, any evaluation of business risks must include an analysis of the current and future economic climate and its influences upon the business. In addition there are some important insurable business hazards that must be considered. These include legal liability, property damage, theft, surety bonds, and life, accident, and health risks.

If a taxpayer's business interests are closely held, special problems arise. These include problems of valuation and liquidity. To effectively analyze the business risks of a closely held firm, the estate owner and his estate-planning team should be knowledgeable of the taxpayer's particular business as well as the economy in general. In valuing the business interests for estate-planning purposes, several factors must be considered. These include the nature and history of the business, conditions in the specific industry as well as the general economic outlook, the financial condition of the organization, the book value of the taxpayer's interests, past earnings, current earnings as well as potential earning ability, dividend policy, and the value of goodwill and other intangibles. To determine if the business can serve as a source of liquidity for the estate, an analysis of the firm's cash flow must be conducted.

Investment Risks

Portfolio management is concerned with investment risks, which are usually classified as purchasing-power risks, interest-rate risks, business risks, and market risks.[5] Where the estate owner has significant investments, some member of the estate-planning team must analyze these holdings with respect to the investment risks and take steps to prevent impairment of the estate if they are considered detrimental. Such steps would include diversification of various kinds and the selection of securities on the basis of their relative invulnerability to depreciation.[6]

Legal Risks

Another type of risk in estate planning, as pointed out by Pfeffer, is lack of legal documentation. Legal risk arises from the failure of the estate owner and his estate-planning team to properly execute the appropriate documents essential to carry out the objectives of the estate owner. All wills, trusts, contracts, and titles to property must be valid and properly executed. These instruments should be prepared by a competent lawyer and then reviewed periodically to assure that they are still in accordance with the desires of the individual. Estate plans that are developed in an atmosphere of ill-defined objectives, procrastination, poorly drawn legal documents, and uncoordinated planning result in unstable designs and legal vulnerability. Much of the ultimate frustration relevant to the legal aspects of estate planning can be avoided by consulting an attorney who is well versed in preventive law.[7]

Tax Risk

An estate owner frequently seeks planning assistance because he is primarily concerned with estate conservation and the effect of taxes on it. Poor or no tax planning can seriously deplete the value of the estate. Many factors having significant tax consequences must be evaluated. These include the differential tax treatment of ordinary versus capital gains income, the two different *effective* tax rates under the single unified-rate structure, of devolution of community versus separate property, estates held in joint tenancy rather than in common, and gifts in contemplation of death versus valid gifts. Another factor having significant tax consequences is the successive taxation of estates when surviving heirs die shortly after the decease of the estate owner.[8]

An evaluation of the tax risks calls for a high degree of skill in the estate-planning process. In order for the estate-planning team to be effective, at least one member must be knowledgeable of the basic provisions of the federal estate and gift tax laws and have an understanding of those sections of the Internal Revenue Code that govern the taxing of income of fiduciaries. Such knowledge is necessary so that protective tax planning can be carried out during the taxpayer's lifetime and be applicable throughout the administration of his estate after his death.

Some member of the estate-planning team should be familiar with the interrelatonships among the federal estate and fiduciary income tax laws. When properly executed, many of these interrelationships allow the administrator to make tax elections that can result in significant overall tax savings to the beneficiaries of the estate. For instance, the value of the assets as shown on the estate tax return may determine the basis of these assets to the beneficiaries for income tax purposes under the fresh-start step-up-in-basis rules. Many other interrelationships between the two taxes must be considered by the administrator (executor or executrix) and the tax adviser.

The inclusion in the decedent's gross estate of a comprehensive range of property and property interests along with the high estate-tax rates magnifies the need for estate planning. Tax planning is not only very important in estate planning, but is also necessary in post-mortem planning. During this time, many decisions have significant effects upon the conservation of the estate, and a proper analysis of available alternatives can result in significant tax savings and help preserve the taxpayer's estate.

Post-Mortem Conservation of Liquid Assets

Several other factors that cause impairment of the estate should be considered by the members of the estate-planning team. One of the most important of these is the liquidity of the assets. Many estates are burdened with debts and obligations; the estate must pay the cost of the last illness, funeral expenses, estate administration expenses, federal and state taxes, and honor the cash bequests of the decedent. Since there must be a sufficient amount of liquid assets to meet these needs, a determination of the liquidity needs of the taxpayer's estate should be made. Using the information obtained during the fact-gathering stage as a guide, the members of the estate-planning team should be able to make rough estimates of these costs. These estimates will help determine the cash requirements of estate disbursements and serve as additional background information for the preparation of the estate plan. If the estate is burdened with a shortage of liquid assets, income-producing assets might have to be sold, possibly for less than their real value, to meet these needs. The dilution of the income-producing assets may have significant adverse effects upon the survivors of the decedent.

Another source of impairment that demands consideration is the instability of the property values of the estate. Changes in consumer preference, obsolescence, or improper management of the estate's assets could cause a severe shrinkage in the value of the estate. Consideration should be given to the possibility of prolonged and expensive illness or disability, loss of income, and legal liability of the estate owner. Insurance should be acquired to help reduce the burden in case one or more of these possibilities occur.[9]

Certainly, the members of the estate-planning team must analyze all factors that could shrink or deplete the value of the taxpayer's estate. However, this evaluation of risks is only one step in the estate-planning process. There are several other steps, which are just as important and which must be performed during the estate-planning process.

DESIGNING THE PLAN

Designing the plan is the next step in the estate-planning process. No meaningful design can be adopted until all the facts have been gathered and the objectives of the estate owner have been determined. It is on these facts and objectives that the plan must be based. To be worthwhile, it must be capable of accomplishing the objectives of the estate owner. This requisite increases the importance of the estate-planning team, for the members of the team, having played the role of investigators, now must use their creative skills and abilities to create an effective plan, one as simple and flexible as possible while still accomplishing its objectives.[10]

A variety of methods exists to help accomplish the objectives of the estate owner. Through analyzing various combinations of these transfers of assets, the ultimate plan is developed. The plan should be tested and the consequences evaluated. No attempt is made in this chapter to mention all the available vehicles of transfer, but a few are discussed below for illustrative purposes.

The Estate Owner's Will

The will is a key vehicle of transfer, and its preparation is often the first step taken by estate owners in planning the disposition of their estates. The will is used to designate heirs, identify the property they are to receive, indicate the person (or institution) who will act as administrator of the estate, and similar details. Some useful provisions attached to this document are the marital deduction and the marital deduction trusts. The basic advantage in using the marital deduction is the favorable tax consequence. The costs of this tax savings, however, may be the compromise of the estate owner's objectives, the possible deferred increase in transfer costs, or the loss of control of an asset.[11]

Under certain conditions and limitations, the estates of citizens and residents of the United States are allowed a marital deduction up to approximately 50 percent of the adjusted gross estate. The purpose of the marital deduction is to eliminate the tax advantages held by those persons domiciled in community-property states. These statutes provide all taxpayers the same tax treatment as that previously available only to the residents of the community-property states.

Trusts

Trusts are another means of transfer. *Inter vivos* and testamentary, revocable and irrevocable, and funded and unfunded trusts may be used by the estate planner. Some of the important advantages of trusts are that they are based on the concepts of property arrangement and property settlement. The main purpose of the trust device is to serve as a means of preserving and administering property for the benefit of the beneficiaries.

Because it permits considerable flexibility in the disposition of property, the trust is one of the most valuable tools in estate planning. It provides the flexibility needed to achieve nontax objectives, such as relieving other family members of responsibility, obtaining competent management of the property, providing discretion in income and principal distributions, and many others. Also advantageous, perhaps equally significant in many instances, are the income and estate tax economies obtainable through the use of trusts.

Trusts are formed for many purposes. A trust may be created to achieve any desired objective, as long as the objective is not illegal or contrary to any policy or rule of law. Some of the more common types of trusts, classified as to purpose, include insurance trusts, educational trusts, support trusts, charitable trusts, and marital deduction trusts.

When a trust is created, it is only natural and proper that the grantor and his estate-planning team should construct it in a way that maximizes the use of the available favorable tax provisions. However, the purpose of its establishment is ordinarily not just to save taxes. The saving of taxes is one reason for the creation of trusts; but the process of carrying out an orderly and sensible disposition of the trust property according to the desires of the estate owner should be the primary reason for its establishment. The new generation-skipping tax must be considered when a trust is established, however.

Life Insurance

Another means of transfer is life insurance, which is often the only practical way of guaranteeing that sufficient cash will be available to meet the financial costs of death. Life insurance has many advantages. In many states its use provides savings in estate taxes. Also, insurance proceeds can be removed from the probate estate, thus reducing probate and administrative costs. In many instances, the greatest advantage of life insurance in estate planning is that it can satisfy the obligations of the estate, thus preventing the forced sale of income-producing assets. In essence, the inclusion of life insurance in the estate plan should be determined by the needs for liquidity, flexibility, tax minimization, investment, and the requirements of family income.[12]

As with other devices of transfer, the estate owner and his advisers should carefully consider the tax consequences of the use of life insurance, which provides many tax advantages.

Annuities

Private annuities represent another important vehicle of transfer. However, careful consideration must be given to the risks involved. In such a contract, the annuitant transfers property other than cash to the obligor in return for the obligor's unsecured promise to make periodic payments of money to the annuitant for a specific period of time. The period of time is usually for the life of the annuitant. Thus, the major risk to the annuitant is the obligor's failure to make the required payments.

Fortunately, the private annuity offers several tax advantages. First, since this is a valid sales contract, the property is removed from the estate of the obligor. Second, IRC Sec. 72 governs the income taxability of the annuity payments. Thus, each payment is broken into three portions: an excluded portion, an ordinary income portion, and a capital gain or loss portion. This gives the annuitant the additional advantage of spreading any gain from the sale of such property over a period of several years for income tax purposes. In essence, it gives the annuitant a deferment for payment of the income taxes associated with the transfer.

Lifetime Gifts

Another effective vehicle of transfer in estate planning is the lifetime gift, which eliminates all probate

and administration expenses on the property transferred. Gifts may reduce estate taxes because the
amount of income that would have been accumulated from the property is removed from the transferor's gross estate. Often the use of a gift provides
savings in income taxes because the income is
shifted from the high-income tax bracket of the
transferor into the low-income bracket of the transferee. Of course, the use of gifts produces many advantages other than taxes. They may be used to continue control of a business within the family or to
serve specific desires the estate owner has for his
children. Gifts, like all other devices, have their
costs; the most significant cost of making a gift is the
complete loss of control of the asset. Of course, with
the new unified tax structure, the use of gifts as an
estate-planning tool has lost some of its glamour.

Before making lifetime gifts, it must be remem-
bered that, under certain circumstances, the gift
property may later be included in the donor's gross
estate along with a gross-up of the gift taxes even
though they were made during the donor's lifetime.
Without adequate and full consideration of this tax
risk, any transfers of property made by the decedent
within three years of death are interpreted as in contemplation of death; thus, such property and gift tax
gross-ups are included in the donor's gross estate.
Likewise, the relinquishment of a power over property transferred during lifetime, or the exercise or
release of a power of appointment, within three
years before death is deemed to have been made in
contemplation of death.

The vehicles of transfer discussed in the preceding paragraphs are only some of those available to

the estate owner. During the design and before the implementation of an estate plan, the members of the estate-planning team must evaluate the advantages and disadvantages of these methods of transfer. The vehicles that aid in the accomplishment of the estate owner's objectives should be incorporated into the estate plan.

IMPLEMENTATION OF THE PLAN

Before the estate plan becomes effective, the appropriate legal documents must be executed. The necessity for careful planning and execution of the legal documents cannot be overemphasized, for faulty execution is a sure way of invalidating the entire efforts of any estate plan. Thus, these legal instruments must be drafted by a competent attorney who is well versed in estate-planning techniques.

These documents must be reviewed periodically to ascertain that they continue to express the objectives of the estate owner. A periodic review of the financial status and other family relationships should be conducted to determine if there have been any changes that necessitate a revision of the estate plan. Also, the plan should be reviewed in the light of any changes or potential changes in the relevant legal or tax aspects. Such a review could bring about a modification in the plan that would produce significant benefits to the estate owner, while the neglect of such a review could be very costly to him.

As can be seen from the preceding discussion of the estate-planning process, many professional skills are required to effectively perform such a service. Usually, a team effort is utilized during the process. The attorney, accountant (CPA), trust officer, and insurance underwriter are the professionals most often associated with the team.

THE ESTATE-PLANNING TEAM

Since estate planning is such a complex and subtle process, a team effort is usually necessary to effectively accomplish the objectives of the estate owner. By virtue of his/her tendency toward salesmanship, the life insurance underwriter is often the prime motivator in interesting prospects in an estate plan that will eventually involve the orchestration of the other members of the estate-planning team. Unlike the lawyer and the accountant, the insurance salesperson has a license to sell, and has a special skill to seek out and solicit new insurance business. Often the life underwriter uncovers situations where only a properly executed estate plan can save a taxpayer's estate from erosion. Also, the insurance underwriter has a specialized knowledge of the many forms of life insurance, and knows what various policies can and cannot do.

The attorney's participation is most essential in determining the legal and tax consequences of every phase in the process of developing an estate plan. The lawyer must determine whether certain recommendations and phases in the formulation of the plan have legal substance and merit. Only a competent attorney can draft the legal documents that provide the framework for the execution of the estate plan.

Estate planning is the trust officer's prime concern, not only because it is a device for developing new business, but also because it constitutes the bulk of the trust department's activities. The trust officer, who is essentially an instrument of estate conservation and management, can lend advice on the practicalities of the plan and play a major role in the administration of the estate. Under a specific agreement, he accepts custody of the property, manages and invests it, and distributes it to the beneficiaries according to the stipulations of the trust instrument.

Normally, the accountant (CPA) is considered to be the member of the estate-planning team who is intimately acquainted with the financial affairs of the taxpayer and is knowledgeable of income and estate tax laws. In addition, the CPA is to advise on valuation problems and to determine the existing and potential earning power of a business. Otherwise, the accountant's role as a member of the estate-planning team is not so easily ascertained or clearly defined as the roles of the other members, but it should be obvious that the accountant's knowledge of the client's affairs should enable him to recognize the client's need of estate-planning services. Therefore, the accountant is the person on the team who has the responsibility to initiate the estate-planning process.

REFERENCES

1. W. H. Hoffman, Jr., *Effective Estate Planning Procedures for Minimizing Taxes.* (Englewood Cliffs, N.J.: Prentice-Hall, Inc., 1968), p. 3.

2. L. J. Ackerman, "Estate Planning Principles," in D. W. Gregg (ed.) *Life and Health Insurance Handbook.* (Homewood, Ill.: Richard D. Irwin, Inc., 1959), p. 498.
3. Irving Pfeffer, "The Nature and Scope of Estate Planning," *California Management Review*, IX (Fall, 1966), p. 26.
4. Ackerman, *op. cit.*, pp. 497–498.
5. Donald E. Vaughn, *Survey of Investments.* (New York: Holt, Rinehart and Winston, Inc., 1967), p. 49.
6. Pfeffer, *op. cit.*, pp. 26–27.
7. *Ibid.*, p. 27.
8. *Ibid.*, p. 27.
9. Ackerman, *op. cit.*, pp. 494–495.
10. *Ibid.*, p. 498.
11. *Ibid.*, p. 499.
12. *Ibid.*, pp. 499–500.

2

What Is Included in Gross Estate?

The legal right of a taxpayer to decrease
the amount of what otherwise would be his taxes,
or altogether avoid them, by means which
the law permits, cannot be doubted.
Justice George Sutherland

THE federal estate tax is an excise tax on the privilege of transferring property at the time of a person's death. This levy is not a property tax or a tax on the right of the beneficiary to receive the property. Unlike a state inheritance tax, the rates are not dependent upon the relationship of the beneficiaries to the decedent. Note that the same unified rate structure also applies to lifetime gifts after 1976.

Since the federal estate tax (like any other liability) dilutes the amount of assets passing to the heirs, many people seek effective ways to reduce this tax burden. However, before an individual can evaluate the diluting effects of federal taxes on assets, he/she must have some familiarity with the basic provisions of the estate tax laws. These laws apply not only to every citizen and resident of this country, but also to any nonresident alien who dies and leaves property located within this country. However, the federal estate tax laws differ between citizens and residents and those who are nonresidents and not citizens. This chapter is concerned only with the statutes that apply to citizens and/or residents of the United States. ·

OVERVIEW OF THE ESTATE TAX LAWS

Basically, the gross estate includes all property owned in whole or in part by the decedent at the time of death. The value of such property is limited to the extent of the decedent's interest in it. Also, the gross estate may include assets that may not be in the probated will. These assets may include property in which the decedent had a general power of appointment, gifts made after December 31, 1976, jointly owned property, dower or curtesy rights of a surviving spouse, revocable transfers made by the decedent, proceeds of certain life insurance policies, and annuities.

In order to determine the decedent's taxable estate, certain deductions are subtracted from the gross estate. Some of the allowable deductions include funeral and administrative expenses, debts of the decedent, taxes, casualty losses, charitable contributions, and a marital deduction for bequests to the spouse.

The appropriate unified estate tax rates are applied to the taxable estate to obtain the gross estate tax. However, in order to determine the net estate tax that is payable, certain authorized credits are subtracted from the gross estate tax. These credits include a credit for state death taxes paid, a credit for tax on prior transfers, a credit for foreign death taxes, and a unified estate and gift tax credit. The Tax Reform Act of 1976 replaced the estate tax exemption of $60,000 and the gift tax exemption of $30,000 with a new unified tax credit. (A credit is a dollar-for-dollar offset against the tax.) This new credit is to be phased in over a five-year period. The amount of the credit is $30,000 in 1977, $34,000 in 1978, $38,000 in 1979, $42,500 in 1980, and $47,000 thereafter. These unified credits are *approximately* equivalent to an exemption of $120,000 in 1977, $134,000 in 1979, $162,000 in 1980, and $175,625 thereafter.

GROSS ESTATE

Before any estimate can project the amount of estate tax to be paid on the death of an individual, one must know what assets are included in the gross estate, and also the value to be placed on them. Without knowledge of these two things, the estate planner is helpless in estimating the potential estate tax.

All property, including real or personal, tangible or intangible, owned in whole or in part by the decedent at the time of death is included in gross estate to the extent of the value of any interest in such property. Until July 1, 1964, the gross estate did not include any real property located outside the United States; however, the law was amended to include such property of all decedents who died after that date. Since the gross estate includes the value of the decedent's interest in all property owned at his/her death, ownership is an important factor in determining the gross estate. Normally, local property law controls the issue of ownership for tax purposes.[1]

Even though the decedent's gross estate is composed of a wide variety of "owned" property, it is *not* limited to "owned" property. The gross estate also includes certain other assets in which the interest of the decedent is considered to be substantially equivalent to ownership, although the decedent held no legal interest in the property at the time of death. Items in this category are discussed below.

Dower or Curtesy Interest

The gross estate of a decedent includes the value of all property passing to the surviving spouse as dower or curtesy or by virtue of a statute creating an estate in lieu of dower and curtesy as determined by the laws of the specific state. A dower (to the wife) or curtesy (to the husband) is a statutory provision in a common-law state which directs a certain portion of the estate to the surviving spouse (often one-third of the estate). However, state law does not determine the tax status of that interest under the federal statute.[2]

Example 1:   Wife is killed in a car accident without a will (that is, intestate), leaving an estate of $900,000. Under the state law, husband is entitled to one-third of the wife's estate. The $300,000 that the husband receives is included in wife's gross estate under Section 2034.

Retained Life Interest

A transfer with a retained life interest is included in the gross estate. Included under this provision is the value of all property or property interest transferred by a decedent, by trust or otherwise, if the decedent retained it for life, or for any period not ascertainable without reference to death, or for a period of time that in fact does not end before the decedent's death. Specifically, under the federal statute, such interest is identified by

1. The possession, right to income, or other enjoyment of the property [Section 2036(a)(1)].

2. The right, either alone or in conjunction with any other person, to designate who shall possess or enjoy the property or the income therefrom [Section 2036(a)(2)].[3]

According to Regulation 20.2036-1, the use, possession, right to the income, or other enjoyment of the property is considered as having been retained by the decedent if it is to be applied to the discharge of any of his legal obligations, including his obligation during his lifetime to support a dependent. The phrase "right . . . to designate the person or persons who shall possess or enjoy the transferred property or the income therefrom" does not apply to a power held solely by a person other than the decedent. But if the decedent reserved the unrestricted power to remove a trustee at any time and appoint himself as trustee, the decedent is considered as having the powers of the trustee.

Example 2: Husband created a trust naming an independent party the trustee. Any income from this trust was to go to his three minor children to be used to help satisfy his obligation to support them. After reaching age 18, the income interests were to continue for each of their lives. At the death of each child, one-third of the trust was to pass to each child's children. Husband died when his children were 12, 15, and 23 years of age. Since two-thirds of the trust income was being used to satisfy the legal obligation of support, two-thirds of the trust assets would be included in husband's gross estate under Section 2036.

Example 3: Husband deeds house to his wife, but continues to live in the home. More than three years later husband dies. As long as there is not an implicit agreement that the husband may live in the house, Section 2036 would not pull the house into the decedent's estate. See *A.D. Gutchess*, 46 T.C. 554 (1966), acq. 1967-1 C.B.2.

Property Transfers

Transfers taking effect at death must be included in the gross estate under Section 2037. The decedent's gross estate must include the value of any interest in property transferred by the decedent in any way, except for an adequate and full consideration in money or money's worth, if all the following conditions are met:

1. Possession or enjoyment of the property could, through ownership of the interest, have been obtained only by surviving the decedent.

2. The decedent has retained a reversionary interest in the transferred property by the expressed terms of the instrument of transfer.

3. The value of the reversionary interest immediately before the death of the decedent exceeds 5 percent of the value of the transferred property.

For purposes of this section, the term "reversionary interest" includes the possibility that property transferred by the decedent may return to him or his estate or may be subject to a power of disposition by him. This term does not include rights to income only. The value of such reversionary interest is determined by the usual methods of valuation, including the use of mortality tables and actuarial principles.[4] In essence, whereas a transfer with a retained life estate (Section 2036) pulls in the entire amount of the property, a transfer taking effect at death (Section 2037) pulls in *some* of the property.

Example 4:   An individual (decedent) transfers property to a trust with the income payable to his wife for life and with the remainder payable to the decedent or, if he is not living at his wife's death, to his daughter or her estate. The daughter could not obtain possession or enjoyment of the property without surviving the decedent. Assuming the decedent's reversionary interest immediately before his death exceeded 5 percent of the value of the property, the value of the property, *less* the value of the wife's outstanding life estate, is includable in the decedent's gross estate under Section 2037.

Revocable transfers are drawn back into the gross estate under Section 2038. Property transferred during the decedent's lifetime is includable in the decedent's gross estate if at the time of his death the enjoyment of the property is subject to change through the exercise of a power to alter, amend, revoke, or terminate by the decedent, either alone or in conjunction with another person.[5] However, according to Regulation 20.2038-1 this provision does not apply (1) to the extent that the transfer was for adequate and full consideration in money or money's worth; (2) if the decedent's power could be exercised only with the consent of all parties having an interest in the transferred property; or (3) to a power held solely by a person other than the decedent.

Example 5:   Husband creates a trust with income to wife or wife's estate for husband's life and remainder to his son or son's estate. Husband, as the trustee, retains a power to give the remainder to his daughter. If husband dies, everything is pulled into his gross estate under Section 2038.

Example 6:   Grantor transfers some securities to his minor daughter (age, two years) under the Model Gifts of Securities to Minors Act. Grantor is the custodian of the stock. Although this is a valid technique for income tax purposes, if the grantor dies before the daughter reaches majority, the securities are included in the grantor's gross estate under Section 2038. Of course, to avoid this unfavorable tax result, someone else should be appointed the custodian (for example, the grantor's spouse).

Annuities

The gross estate includes the value of an annuity or other payment receivable by a beneficiary by reason of surviving the decedent under any form of contract or agreement, including employment plans and agreements (except life insurance contracts) when the value of the annuity or other payment is attributable to contributions made by the decedent or his employer if (1) the payment or annuity was payable to the decedent, or (2) the decedent possessed the right to receive such annuity or payment, either alone or in conjunction with another, for his life or for any period not ascertainable without reference to his death, or for any period that does not in fact end before his death.[6]

The amount included in the gross estate under such a contract is limited to the part of the value of the annuity receivable that is proportionate to the part of the purchase price contributed by the decedent's employer. For this purpose, any contribution made by the decedent's employer or former employer as a consequence of his employment is considered as being contributed by the decedent. There is excluded, however, the value of annuities or other benefits receivable by a beneficiary (other than the estate) under certain "qualified" employee benefit plans. This exclusion applies only to the benefits attributable to the employer's contributions.[7] Further, an annuity that terminates at the decedent's death (that is, single-life, nonrefund annuity) is not included in the decedent's gross estate.

Example 7: Husband enters into a contract with an insurance company under which he paid the company

$100,000 and his wife paid $50,000 from her funds. The company agreed that in 1982 they would pay husband $200 per month for life, and after his death the company would make like payment to his wife for life. Husband dies in 1980, survived by wife. Two-thirds of the value of the annuity would be included in husband's estate under Section 2039(b).

Power of Appointment

The value of all property over which the decedent possessed a *general* power of appointment at the time of his death is includable in his gross estate. A *general* power of appointment is one under which the holder has the right to dispose of the property in favor of (1) himself, (2) his estate, (3) his creditors, or (4) the creditors of his estate. In essence, if one should exercise a general power of appointment during lifetime, there is a taxable gift. But if the general power is held at death, the property is included in the gross estate under Section 2041.

There are some exceptions to this definition of a *general* power of appointment:

1. When the holder's right to consume or invade the property is limited by an ascertainable standard relating to his needs for health, maintenance, support, or education, the power is not considered to be a general power of appointment.

2. If power created on or before October 21, 1942, is exercisable by the decedent only in conjunction with another person, it is not general.

3. If power created after October 21, 1942, is exercisable by the decedent only in conjunction with the creator of the power or with a person hav-

ing substantial interest in the property subject to the power in the decedent's favor, it is excluded.

4. If the power may be exercised both in favor of the decedent and the persons whose consent the decedent must have, the power is general to the extent of the decedent's fractional interest in it.[8]

A general power is different from a *special* power of appointment. A special power of appointment may appoint anyone other than the four parties mentioned above. An individual may hold a special power of appointment at death and not include the property in the gross estate.

Example 8: Decedent was granted a life estate in a trust with a power to invade corpus as desired in order to continue an accustomed standard of living. Since decedent possessed a power that was not limited by an ascertainable standard relating to health, education, support, or maintenance, decedent possessed a general power of appointment and the property would be included in his gross estate under Section 2041.

Example 9: Decedent has a general power of appointment created in 1968 by grantor. However, decedent has the right to appoint all of the corpus of the trust to anyone, but only with the consent of Harvey. After decedent's death, Harvey alone will have the power to appoint corpus of the trust to anyone. Since Harvey can wait and get all of the trust (that is, an adverse interest), the trust corpus is not included in decedent's estate under Section 2041(b)(1)(c)(ii).

Life Insurance

Proceeds of insurance on the decedent's life, receivable by or for the benefit of the estate or by other beneficiaries, are included in the gross estate of the decedent under Section 2042. Life insurance, for estate tax purposes, includes not only the common forms of insurance taken out by an individual upon his life but also the proceeds of certain other types of policies including accident insurance, war risk insurance, and group insurance. Life insurance payable to named beneficiaries is subject to special rules. The proceeds of such a policy are included in the gross estate only if the decedent possessed at his death any incidents of ownership in the policy or certain reversionary interests.

The term "reversionary interest" includes the possibility that the policy or the proceeds of the policy may return to the decedent or his estate. For the proceeds of the policy to be included in the decedent's gross estate, the value of such reversionary interest must exceed 5 percent of the value of the policy immediately before the death of the decedent. The value of a reversionary interest is determined by the usual methods of valuation, including the use of mortality tables and actuarial principles.[9]

Real Property Interests

There are various types of joint ownership of property. *Tenancy by the entirety* with rights of survivorship occurs between a husband and wife. *Joint tenancy* with rights of survivorship occurs between nonspouses. Before 1977, under both arrangements, each party was viewed as owning all under Section 2040. A *tenancy in common* (without rights of survivorship) is an undivided interest that can be transferred during life or at death. At death the applicable portion of the undivided interest is included in gross estate under Section 2033. *Community property* occurs in seven states where each spouse is viewed as having a one-half vested property right. At death, one-half of the community property is included in the gross estate under Section 2033.

Under prior law the gross estate included 100 percent of the value of all property owned in joint tenancy with rights of survivorship. However, if any part of the property or its acquisition cost is traceable to the survivor, that portion of the value of the property may be excluded from the gross estate. For example, any property acquired jointly by the decedent and another joint owner through a gift is included in the decedent's gross estate only to the extent of the decedent's fractional share of such property. These rules applied to all classes of property, whether real or personal, but did not apply to property held as tenants in common.

The Tax Reform Act of 1976 changed these rules for joint tenancies created after 1976 if the tenants are husband and wife. Under this new law only 50 percent of the value of the tenancy by the entirety is included in the gross estate regardless of which spouse furnished the consideration. For the above rules to apply, the following additional requirements must be met:

1. The joint interest must have been created by one or both of the joint-tenant spouses.
2. If the interest is of personal property, the creation of the joint tenancy must constitute a completed gift and be so shown on a gift tax return.
3. If the interest is of real property, the donor spouse must have elected to treat the creation

of the joint tenancy as a taxable gift at the time.[10]

A point of interest is that these new rules do not apply to the creation of a joint bank account. A gift occurs only when a noncontributing party withdraws money from the joint bank account.

The new rules regarding joint tenancies apply only to such tenancies created *after* December 31, 1976. If local law allows an existing joint tenancy to be severed and recreated after December 31, 1976, the new joint tenancy is eligible under the new rules, provided all conditions discussed above are met.

Example 10:   Husband and wife purchase a piece of real property as tenancy by the entirety for $600,000 *after* 1976. Husband furnished $400,000 and wife furnished $200,000 of the purchase price. The property is worth $800,000 when the wife dies. If no election was made under Section 2515(c), $266,667 is included in wife's gross estate (2/6 × $800,000). If an election was made under Section 2515(c), recognizing a $100,000 taxable gift, $400,000 would be included in wife's estate.

Gifts

For estates of decedents dying after December 31, 1976, the gross estate must also include the amount of all taxable gifts made after December 31, 1976, and within three years of the decedent's death. The amount to be added is the gross amount of the gift less the $3,000 annual exclusion plus gift tax (if any) paid on the transfer (so-called gross-up of the gift tax).[11] This is another new rule added by the

Reform Act of 1976, and its purpose is to eliminate the gifts-in-contemplation-of-death problems experienced under the old law. If the donor died within three years of making the gift, there was a rebuttable presumption that the gift was made in contemplation of death. Also, before 1977, there was no gross-up of the gift-tax liability.

In essence, under the new law, both the gift and the gift-tax liability attributable to the transfer must be included in the estate. This gross-up mechanism does not apply to gifts made more than three years before death or to any gift tax paid by a decedent within three years of death and which is treated as being paid one-half by each spouse under the gift-splitting provision of Section 2513.

Even when it appears that a gift may be made in contemplation of death, such a gift may be worthwhile. The donor might live three years or more and then there would be no transfer tax on any appreciation that occurred between the time of the gift and the donor's death. If the donor dies within three years, he may be in a high-income tax bracket, and then the transfer would place the income-producing property in the hands of a lower-tax-bracket donee.

Example 11:   Decedent obtained a life insurance policy on his life which had a face value of $125,000. He paid premiums on it for eight years. In the ninth year he transferred it to his sister. The sister paid two years of premiums, and the decedent retained no incidents of ownership. Decedent died two years after this transfer in 1978. Since the transfer was a gift in contemplation of death, eight-tenths of the $125,000 face value of the policy is included in the decedent's estate.

Miscellaneous Assets

Section 2033 of the Internal Revenue Code requires the inclusion in the decedent's estate of a wide variety of property interests owned by him on the date of his death. Regulation 20.2033-1, and many court cases, have applied this section to many specific items of property interest. According to this regulation, property subject to homestead or other exemptions under local law must be included in the gross estate. Notes or other claims held by the decedent should be included even though they are canceled by his will. Accrued interest and rents are includable even though they are not collected until after his death, and under certain circumstances dividends payable to the decedent are included. Bonds, notes, bills, and certificates of indebtedness of the federal government or its agencies, which are exempt from other taxes, are subject to the estate tax and are included in the decedent's gross estate. The tax treatments of many other particular property interests are covered, and some of these are discussed below.

As a general rule, accrued income, dividends, interest, compensation, and other items accrued at the time of the decedent's death should be included in his gross estate. However, this rule does not apply if any of these types of payments are made only as a matter of grace.[12] The following accruals have been held includable in the decedent's estate:

1. Executor's fees accrued at the date of the decedent's death.[13]
2. Accrued interest on the decedent's capital investment in a partnership.[14]

3. Accrued interest on Series G Bonds even though they were held under six months.[15]
4. Salary and bonus paid under contract to the decedent's widow by employer.[16]
5. Commission.[17]
6. Dividends.[18]
7. Bonus.[19]
8. Partnership profits.[20]

For estate tax purposes, dividends accrue to the stockholder on the date of the record date. Thus, dividends that are payable to the decedent or his estate constitute a part of the gross estate if, on or before the date of his death, the decedent was the stockholder of record. If the record date is after the date of death, the dividends are not included in the gross estate. This rule applies no matter how the gross estate is valued. However, if the record date is after the valuation date and the stock is selling ex-dividend on the valuation date, the dividend is added to the quotation to obtain the includable value of the stock.[21]

Any bonus paid to the decedent's estate or to a named beneficiary may be subject to tax as an accrual. However, the bonus is not included if the employer is under no duty to make the payment.[22]

Like any other accrual, partnership profits to date of death of the decedent are included in his gross estate.[23] In some instances, profits accruing after the partner's death are included in his gross estate.[24] If a partnership agreement stipulates that the deceased partner's estate is to share in the profits for a definite period of time after death, then such profits accruing to the estate are included in the gross estate.[25]

Any property owned as a tenancy in common is included in the decedent's gross estate to the extent of his fractional interest in such property.[26] Even cemetery lots are included in the decedent's gross estate under certain circumstances. If any part of a cemetery lot not designed for the interment of the decedent and the members of his family has a salable value, then that salable value is included in his gross estate.[27]

All valid and enforceable claims or choses in action owned by the decedent are included in his gross estate. The following types of claims and choses in action are includable: right to executor's commissions,[28] contingent-fee . legal services,[29] debts due the decedent,[30] trustee's commission,[31] claims against a partner,[32] computed value of claim for advance,[33] and others. Any notes held by the decedent are included in his gross estate unless the obligations end on death.[34]

Depending upon the nature of the payment, death benefits provided for in pension or profit-sharing plans may or may not be included in the decedent's gross estate. Even though the decedent had the right to appoint his share of the fund to his beneficiaries, the proceeds paid from such a trust fund are not included in his gross estate if the decedent did not have a vested interest in the fund.[35] If he had an enforceable vested interest in such a fund to his beneficiaries, this is included in his gross estate.[36]

Cases, revenue ruling, and income tax regulation apply Section 2033 of the Internal Revenue Code to many more miscellaneous items of property and property interest. These situations are too numerous to discuss in detail, but most of the important ones have been briefly covered.

REFERENCES

1. *Internal Revenue Code of 1954.* (The remaining footnotes from the Internal Revenue Code of 1954 will be cited as Sections 2031, 2033, etc.)
2. Section 2034.
3. Reg. 20.2036-1(b)(3) seems to override the Code by striking the phrase "or the income" from Section 2036(a)(2). This regulation was held valid in *Farrell* v. *U.S.*, CCT.CL. (1977).
4. Section 2037.
5. Section 2038.
6. Section 2039(a).
7. Section 2039(b), (c).
8. Section 2041.
9. Section 2042.
10. Section 2040.
11. Section 2001.
12. *Maas Exec. (Sakas) et al.* v. *Higgins,* 312 U.S. 443 (1941), 61 S. Ct. 631, 85LL. Ed. 940, 25 AFTR 1177.
13. *Est. of Percy McGlue,* 41 BTA 1199 (1940).
14. *Est. of John F. Degener,* 26 BTA 185 (1932).
15. *Est. of Willis L. King, Jr. (Mellon Nat. Bank & Trust Co.),* 18 TC 414 (1949).
16. *Est. of Paul G. Leoni,* 48, 213 P-H Memo TC (1948).
17. *Est. of Harry Eliot Robinson,* 42, 018 P-H Memo BTA.
18. Revenue Ruling 54-399, 1954-2 C.B. 279; *Estate of George McNought Lockie,* 21 TC 64 (1952).
19. *Est. of Leonard B. McKitterick,* 42 BTA 130, dismissed (2 Cir.; 1941).
20. *Bull, Exec.* v. *U.S.*, 295 U.S. 247 (1935), 55 S. Ct. 695, 15 AFTR 1069, rev'g 6 F. Supp. 141, 13 AFTR 262 (1934).
21. Revenue Ruling 54-399, 1954-2 C.B. 279; *Estate of George McNought Lockie,* 21 TC 64 (1952).

22. *Est. of Leonard B. McKitterick,* 42 BTA 130, dismissed (2 Cir.; 1941).
23. *Supra,* Note 8.
24. *Est. of George Wood,* 26 BTA 533 (1932); *Est. of John F. Degener,* 26 BTA 185 (1932).
25. Revenue Ruling 66-20, 1966-1 C.B. 214.
26. *Harvey, Exr. v. U.S.,* 185 F. 2d 463 (7 Cir.; 1950).
27. Regulation 20.2033-1(b).
28. *Est. of G. Perry McGlue,* 41 BTA 1199 (1940).
29. Rev. Rul. 55-123, C.B. 1955-1 443.
30. *Est. of Heran F. Hammor,* 10 BTA 43 (1928).
31. *Est. of Harry Eliot Robinson,* 42, 018 P-H Memo BTA.
32. *Isaac W. Baldwin Est.,* 59, 203 P-H Memo TC (1959).
33. *Est. of Theodore O. Hamlin (Lincoln Rochester Tr. Co.),* 9 TC 676 (1947).
34. *Comm. v. Austin,* 73 F. 2d 483, 43 AFTR 748 (1934).
35. *Hamner v. Glenn,* 212 F. 2d 483 (6 Cir.; 1954).
36. *Est. of Charles B. Wolf,* 29 TC 441 (1957), 3 AFTR 2d 1797.

3

Valuing
the Gross Estate

The thing generally raised on land is taxes.
Will Rogers

ONCE a determination has been made of what
property should be included in the gross estate, a
value must be assigned to each of these items of
property. There are three major options available
for valuing items of property: fair market value, alternate valuation, and special use valuation. Each of
these options is discussed below in relation to the
tax basis to beneficiaries. Generally, all assets must
be valued at their fair market value at the date of
death or on the alternate valuation date. Fair market

value is normally defined as the price at which the property would change hands between a willing buyer and a willing seller, neither being under any compulsion to buy or sell and both having knowledge of all relevant facts.

FAIR MARKET VALUE

The fair market value is never determined by a forced sale price or by the sale of the item in a market other than that in which the item is most commonly sold. Therefore, if a particular item of property is normally retailed, the fair market value of the item to be included in the decedent's gross estate is the price at which the item or a comparable item would be sold at retail.

For example, an automobile is generally retailed; thus, its fair market value would be the price at which a similar automobile could be purchased by a member of the general public, and is not the price for which the particular automobile of the decedent would be purchased by a dealer in used cars. The selling price of tangible personal property sold at a public auction or through newspaper classified advertising will be deemed the retail price for estate tax purposes. To qualify, the sale must be made within a reasonable period following the applicable valuation date, when there is no substantial change in market conditions or other circumstances affecting the value of similar items between the time of sale and the applicable valuation date. Further, for estate tax purposes, property shall not be valued at the value at which it is assessed for local tax purposes unless that assessed value represents the fair market value on the applicable valuation date.[1]

In determining the fair market value of any item of property, all the relevant facts and elements of value on the valuation date must be considered. The following paragraphs discuss the normal means of valuing particular types of property.

Stocks and Bonds

Stocks and bonds are included in the decedent's gross estate at their fair market value per share or per bond on the valuation date. This fair market value is the mean value between the highest and lowest selling prices on the date of valuation. When there are sales on dates within a reasonable period of time, both before and after the valuation date but no sale on the valuation date, the fair market value is the weighted average of the means between the highest and lowest sales on the nearest dates both before and after the valuation date. This average should be weighted inversely by the respective numbers of trading days between the valuation date and the nearest selling dates. If there are no actual sales within a reasonable period of time of the valuation date, then the fair market value is considered to be the mean between the bona fide and asked prices on the date of valuation.

If it can be established that the value of such stocks and bonds determined on the basis of selling prices or on bid-and-asked prices does not reflect the fair market value, then other relevant facts and elements must be considered in determining the fair market value. For example, if the block of stock were so large in relation to actual sales on the existing market that it could not be liquidated in a reasonable time without depressing the market, or if the block represents a controlling interest, then the price at which other lots change hands may have little relation to the true market value.[2]

If no actual sales prices or bona fide bid-and-asked prices exist, then other factors must be considered in determining the fair market value. In the case of bonds, the soundness of the security, the interest yield, the date of maturity, and other relevant factors must be considered. The factors to consider in the case of shares of stock are the company's net worth, prospective earnings, dividend paying capacity, and other relevant factors. Some of the other relevant factors are goodwill of the business, the economic outlook of the industry, the company's position within the industry, and, of course, its management capability.[3]

There is no theoretical standard or general formula for valuing stock of closely held corporations or any other unlisted stock. The factors to be considered in determining the value of such stock vary with the particular facts involved. The weight to be given to any factor depends upon the specific circumstances of that case. The following fundamental factors should receive careful analysis in every case:

1. The nature of the business and the history of the enterprise from its inception.
2. The economic outlook in general, and the condition and outlook of the specific industry in particular.
3. The book value of the stock and the financial condition of the business.

4. The earning capacity of the company.
5. The dividend-paying capacity.
6. Whether or not the enterprise has goodwill or other intangible value.
7. Sales of the stock and the size of the block to be valued.
8. The market price of stocks of corporations engaged in the same or a similar line of business and having their stocks actively traded in a free and open market, either as an exchange or over the counter.[4]

Business Interests

The fair market value of a decedent's interest in any business is the net amount a willing buyer would pay a willing seller for such interest, neither being under any compulsion to buy or to sell, and both having reasonable knowledge of all the facts. A fair appraisal should be made of the earning capacity of the business and of all its assets, including goodwill. These elements should be considered in determining its net value.[5] However, the value of a business interest may be fixed by a mutual "buy and sell" agreement. For such an agreement to be effective for estate tax purposes, it must bind the estate to sell, either by giving the survivors an option or by binding all parties, and the price must not be so grossly inadequate as to make the agreement a "mere gratuitous promise." [6]

Cash Accounts

All cash belonging to the decedent, including that in the possession of others and that deposited in banks, is included in his/her gross estate. The bank account may be reduced by valid and bona fide checks that are outstanding on the date of death, but which are subsequently honored by the bank.[7] The fair market value of any secured or unsecured note held by the decedent is presumed to be the principal face amount of the note plus interest accrued to the date of death. Under certain circumstances the executor may establish that the value of the note is something less or even worthless.[8]

Personal Property

Generally, the fair market value of the decedent's household and personal effects is considered to be the price that a willing buyer would pay to a willing seller. There should be a room-by-room itemization of these articles. A separate value should be listed for each item; however, all articles in a room worth $100 or less may be grouped. Instead of making such an itemized list, the executor may, under the penalties of perjury, submit a written statement containing the aggregate value of the property as appraised by a competent appraiser. But, if there are included among these household and personal effects any articles having an artistic or intrinsic value of more than $3,000, the appraisal of an expert must be filed with the estate tax return. Before the executor may sell or distribute any of the household or personal effects in advance of an investigation by an officer of the Internal Revenue Service, he must give to the district director notice of such action. This notice must be accompanied by an appraisal of such property.[9]

Annuities, Insurance, and Other Term Contracts

The fair market value of annuities, life estates, terms for years, remainders, and reversions is their present value. The regulations provide tables to be used in calculating the present value of these assets.[10] The value of a contract for the payment of an annuity or an insurance policy on the life of another person is the price for which such a contract could be acquired on the date of the decedent's death from a company regularly engaged in selling contracts of that character. If further premiums are to be paid on a life insurance policy on the life of another person, the value of such a policy may be approximated by adding to the interpolated terminal reserve at the date of the decedent's death the proportionate part of the gross premium that was last paid before the decedent's death and that covers the period extending beyond that date.[11]

ALTERNATE VALUATION

Although all property belonging to the decedent on the date of his death is included in his gross estate and is generally appraised at its fair market value, the executor may elect to value the estate either at the date of the decedent's death or as of the date six months from date of death. This latter date is referred to as the *alternate valuation date.*

If the alternate valuation date (AVD) is to be used, the executor must make such an election on the estate tax return. In no case may such an election be made or a previous election changed after the date of the tax return. When the AVD is elected, it applies to all property of the gross estate, and is valued according to the following rules:

1. Any property distributed, sold, exchanged, or otherwise disposed of within six months after the decedent's death must be valued as of the date on which it is disposed.

2. Any property not distributed, sold, exchanged, or otherwise disposed of within six months after the decedent's death must be valued as of the date six months after the decedent's death.

3. Any property, interest, or estate that is affected by a mere lapse of time must be valued as of the date of the decedent's death. However, it must be adjusted for any change in value *not due to a mere lapse of time* within six months after the decedent's death or as of the date of its disposition, whichever occurs first.[12]

Of course the purpose of the alternative valuation date is to permit a reduction in estate taxes whenever there is a shrinkage in the aggregate value of the estate property. However, there are some interrelated income tax consequences that should be evaluated before selecting the most advantageous valuation date, especially since the alternative valuation date may not be elected unless the value of the gross estate *at the time of death* exceeds $175,000.

Example 1:   Decedent's gross estate at the date of death is $170,000, but its value six months later is $180,000. There would probably be no estate tax whether or not the alternative valuation date (AVD) election were made. Thus, for purposes of a possible fresh-start stepped-up-basis (see the next section), the executor would probably wish to elect AVD, but Reg. 20.2032-1 (b) (1) apparently nullifies this alternative.

Even when a decedent's will directs the executor to sell assets to a specified individual for less than an adequate and full consideration, the assets are includable in the decedent's gross estate at their fair market value on the applicable valuation date.

SPECIAL-USE VALUATION

For estates of decedents dying after December 31, 1976, a "special-use valuation" is available in the case of property being used for farming purposes or closely held businesses.[13] Any property so qualified may be valued at the fair market value of its actual use rather than any speculative value (that is, "highest and best" use) that it might have. This special valuation process may be used to reduce the value of an estate up to $500,000.[14] For example, if a decedent's estate contains special-use property that is valued at $2,300,000 at its "highest and best" use, but only at $1,200,000 at its "current use," the estate would be valued at $1,800,000 ($2,300,000 less $500,000).

In order to qualify for this "special-use valuation," several tests must be met:

1. The value of the closely held business or farm must be at least 50 percent of the gross estate (determined on the basis of its "highest and best" use).
2. The value of the real property must be 25 percent of the gross estate.

3. The property must be located in the United States.
4. The property must pass to a qualified heir.
5. The real property must have been used by the decedent as a farm or other closely held business, and the decedent must have participated materially in its operation during five out of the eight years preceding his death.[15]

The formula for computing this current special-use value may be shown as follows:

$$SUV = \frac{R - T}{I}$$

where SUV = current special-use value

R = average annual gross cash rent per acre for comparable farming land in the same locality

T = average annual state and local real estate taxes per acre for comparable land

I = average annual effective interest rate for all new federal bank loans

There is no "special-use valuation" for purposes of valuing property for the lifetime gift provision.

Example 2: A farmer died in 1978, meeting all the requirements necessary to qualify for the special-use valuation. The highest and best-use value of his 1,000 acre farm is $2.4 million. The average annual gross cash rental per acre is $140, and the average annual state and local real estate taxes per acre are $60. The average annual effective interest rate for all new Federal Land Bank loans is 8 percent. Thus, under the special-use valuation, the land is worth $1,000 per acre ($140 − 60/8% = $1,000). Therefore, the value of the farm as determined under the special-use valuation is $1 million, but under no circumstances may this special method reduce the decedent's estate by more than $500,000. Therefore, the farm would be valued at $1.9 million ($2.4 − 0.5).

TAX BASIS TO BENEFICIARIES

For the years after 1976 there is generally a carry-over basis for property received by a beneficiary (so-called carry-over basis property). Property no longer receives a step-up-in-basis, as was the situation before 1977. However, the basis of property acquired from a decedent dying after December 31, 1976, may be stepped up, in general, to the extent of any appreciation *before* 1977. Marketable bonds and securities are stepped up to their fair market value as of December 31, 1976. A listing of market quotations for bonds and securities as of December 31, 1976, is essential for many years to come.

Example 3:   Decedent owned one share of Woods, Inc., when he died on January 1, 1982. He had purchased the stock on March 17, 1967, for $200 per share. The fair market value (FMV) of the stock at death was $400; the FMV on December 31, 1976, was $300. If this stock was sold by his heir for $390, the heir would have a $90 gain ($390 − 300). If instead, the heir sold the stock for $285, there would be neither a gain nor loss.

The amount of the appreciation occurring prior to 1977 in property other than marketable bonds and securities is determined by multiplying a *ratio* by the total amount of appreciation occurring over the entire period during which a taxpayer is treated as holding the asset. This ratio is calculated by dividing the number of days that the asset has been held by the decedent before 1977 by the total number of days that the taxpayer held the property. In essence, with the new carry-over basis rule, there is less incentive to keep appreciated assets until death. In fact, there may be an incentive for a "sale in contemplation of death," since the gross estate will be less, due to the tax payments on the sale.

Example 4:   An individual acquires a valuable gem on June 30, 1970, at a cost of $500. Suppose the individual dies on May 31, 1979, when the gem is worth $1,000. The fresh-start step-up-in-basis available to the heir would be calculated as follows:

Step 1: Calculate total appreciation of $500
($1,000 − $500)

Step 2: Calculate applicable ratio of 73 percent
$$\frac{\text{number of days before 1977}}{\text{total number of days held}} = \frac{2,375}{3,257} = 0.73$$

Step 3: Multiply ratio by total appreciation
($500 × 0.73 = $365)

Step 4: Determine fresh-start basis to heir of the gem
($500 + 365 = $865)

Thus, the heir would obtain a new tax basis of $865 for the gem, which means that $365 of appreciation income has escaped the income tax forever. Remember that any property purchased *after* December 31, 1976, will have a carry-over basis of cost (that is, the heir "steps into the shoes" of the decedent).

If the decedent's basis in his carry-over basis property is unknown, the heir should use the fair market value of such property as of the date (or approximate date) at which the property was acquired by the decedent or by the last preceding owner in whose hands it did not have a basis in whole or in part by reference to its basis in the hands of a prior holder. Thus, individuals must keep fairly detailed inventory records of their assets. An inventory listing on the schedules reprinted in the Appendix is essential.

A combination of the fresh-start step-up-in-basis and the alternative valuation election can result in income tax savings, as illustrated in the next example.

Example 5: Husband dies on June 1, 19X8, holding (along with other taxable assets) considerable real estate. His adjusted cost basis of the real estate was $500,000. Upon his death, the real estate was worth $1 million, and six months later it was worth $1.1 million. Assume that years later when the real estate was sold, 80 percent of the appreciation occurred before January 1, 1977. If the alternative valuation date is not elected, the carry-over basis to the beneficiary would be $900,000 [$500,000 + (80% × $500,000)]. On the other hand, if the alternative valuation date is elected, the carry-over basis would be $980,000 [$400,000 + (80% × $600,000)]. Thus, this extra $80,000 stepped-up basis eventually escapes the income tax. Note, however, that there is the loss to the beneficiaries of the additional estate tax payable (if any) as a result of the increase in the gross estate income.

Thus, any assets that have increased in value before 1977 (especially if the taxpayer is elderly) should be retained until death so that the heirs will receive the fresh-start step-up-in-basis. An inventory of assets and other property as of December 31, 1976, should be prepared, with records to substantiate the tax basis of each item and the date purchased.

In the absence of any fresh-start step-up-in-basis, assets that have appreciated greatly should be given to beneficiaries who are in low-income tax brackets. Conversely, assets that have not appreciated should be given to beneficiaries in the high-tax bracket.

Before 1977 the death of an individual eliminated any potential depreciation recapture. Regs. 1.1245-2(c)(1)(iv) and 1.1250-3(b)(2) indicated that the depreciation adjustment acquired from a decedent was zero, assuming the basis was determined under Section 1014(a). The new Section 1023 will no longer eliminate any depreciation recapture. Instead, the beneficiary will "step into the shoes of the decedent" and the depreciation recapture will "strike" the beneficiary when and if the beneficiary disposes of the particular asset.

Investment credit property is treated more favorably. Under Reg. 1.47−3(b)(1) there is no investment credit recapture when the estate or beneficiary disposes of the assets that would have given the decedent an investment credit recapture.

Aside from the fresh-start step-up-in-basis, there are several other basis adjustments in Section 1023:

1. A Subsection (c) adjustment for federal or state estate taxes allocable to net appreciation of "appreciated carry-over basis property."

2. The Subsection (d) adjustment allows a $60,000 aggregate minimum basis for all carry-over basis property.

3. There is a Subsection (e) adjustment for state succession taxes actually paid by a transferee of the assets.

4. An executor may elect to exclude up to $10,000 fair market value (FMV) of personal and household property from the carry-over basis rule (that is, such property can be increased to $10,000).

Example 6: Decedent purchased household furniture in May, 1977, for a total cost of $5,000. He dies on January 18, 1984, when the furniture has an FMV of $1,000. If the furniture is sold at a gain for $6,000, only a $1,000 gain would be recognized ($6,000 − $5,000). If instead, the furniture is sold at a price of $3,000 (a loss situation), no gain or loss is recognized.

REFERENCES

1. Reg. 20.2031-1(b).
2. Reg. 20.2031-2(a)-(e).
3. Reg. 20.2031(f).
4. Rev. Ruling 59-60, 1959-1 C.B. 237.
5. Reg. 20.2031-3.
6. Rev. Ruling 59-60, 1959-1 C.B. 237.
7. Reg. 20.2031-5.
8. Reg. 20.2031-4.
9. Reg. 20.2031-6.
10. Reg. 20.2031-7.
11. Reg. 20.2031-8.
12. Section 2032.
13. Section 2032A(a).
14. Section 2032A(a)(2).
15. Section 2032(A)(b).

4

Reductions in Gross Estate

A taxpayer is someone who doesn't
have to take a civil service examination
to work for the government.
Anonymous

A number of reductions—deductions and credits—
are allowed in arriving at the estate tax liability of a
decedent. An intermediate step in the calculation of
the tax liability is "taxable estate."

ALLOWABLE DEDUCTIONS

The taxable estate is the gross estate reduced by all
allowable deductions. Some are discussed below.

Administration and Funeral Expenses

A deduction is granted to the extent allowable under local law for funeral expenses. Funeral expenses include a reasonable expenditure for a tombstone, monument, burial lot, and the cost of transportation of the person taking the body to the place of burial.[1]

All reasonable and necessary expenses incurred in the administration of the decedent's estate are deductible from the gross estate. The administration of the estate includes the collection of the assets, the payment of debts, and the distribution of property to the proper beneficiaries. The three types of administrative expenses are executor's commissions, attorney's fees, and miscellaneous expenses. A deduction for executor's commissions is allowed to the extent that such an amount has actually been paid or for an amount which at the time of the filing of the estate tax return may reasonably be expected to be paid, but no deduction is allowed if the commission is not collected. When the executor is also a major beneficiary, he may wish not to receive a commission because it is taxable as ordinary income. Instead, the executor may wish to receive a larger share of inheritance, which is not taxable to the executor.

Legal Cost Deductions

Attorney fees actually paid or reasonably expected to be paid are deductible. These attorney's fees do not include charges incurred by beneficiaries incident to litigation as to their respective interest. Miscellaneous administrative expenses include court costs, surrogate's fees, clerk hire, and similar charges. All expenses necessarily incurred in preserving and distributing the estate are deductible, including the cost of storing or maintaining property of the estate, when immediate distribution to the beneficiaries is impossible.[2] Expenditures that are not essential for the proper settlement of the estate, but which are incurred for the individual benefit of heirs, legatees, or devisees, are *not* deductible (for example, broker's commission on sale of house by surviving spouse because house is too large). Under Section 642(g), expenditures may not be used to offset the sales price of assets for *income* tax purposes unless a waiver of the right to deduct such item on the federal *estate* tax return is filed.

A deduction is allowed for all bona fide and legally enforceable claims against the estate for debts incurred by the decedent, to the extent paid from property included in the gross estate. Thus, any income or gift taxes owed at the date of death would be deductible under this provision. Also, a deduction is allowed from the decedent's gross estate for the full unpaid amount of a mortgage or other indebtedness with respect to any property included in the gross estate at its full fair market value. This deduction includes an amount for interest accrued to the date of the decedent's death.[3]

Post-Mortem Planning

Post-mortem planning is possible with administrative expenses. An executor may elect to claim certain administrative expenses and medical expenses, either as a deduction on the federal estate tax return (Form 706) or as a deduction in computing the estate income tax (Form 1041). If the executor elects to claim the deduction on Form 1041, he must file a waiver of the deduction for federal estate tax purposes (Form 706).[4]

The value of the gross estate is reduced by any losses incurred during the settlement of the estate arising from fire, storms, thefts, or other casualty. The amount of this deduction is limited to the losses not compensated for by insurance or otherwise under Section 2054.

Any bequest, legacy, or devise made to certain religious, charitable, scientific, education organizations, or to the United States, any state, or political subdivision is deductible. Unlike the charitable deduction for income tax purposes, there are no percentage limitations, and the payment does not have to be made to domestic organizations.[5]

MARITAL DEDUCTIONS

Under certain conditions and limitations, the estates of citizens and residents of the United States are allowed a marital deduction, which is the larger of two amounts: $250,000 or up to 50 percent of the adjusted gross estate under Section 2056(c)(1). This $250,000 figure is subject to two reductions. First, a community-property adjustment under Section 2056(c)(1)(c) reduces this figure by the "excess of the community-property" [a figure defined in Section 2056(c)(2)(B)] that must be deducted from 50 percent of the adjusted gross estate, after deducting the excess of the total expenses under Sections 2053 and 2054 over the actual Sections 2053 and 2054 deductions under the rule applicable to 50 percent of the adjusted gross income in separate community-property states. Second, a reduction is required under Section 2056(c)(1)(B) for certain gift deductions claimed by the decedent (see the discussion in the next section).

The first of these adjustments may be calculated as follows (the maximum marital deduction here is the greater of items 1 and 2(d) below):

1. 50% of adjusted gross estate limitation
   (AGE) $_____
2. $250,000 limitation:
   (a) Maximum $250,000
   (b) Less community-property adjustment:
       (i) Community-property in
           gross estate [Section
           2056(a)(1)(a)] $_____
       (ii) Less related Sections
            2053 and 2054 expenses $_____
   (c) Community-property
       adjustment $_____
   (d) Resulting limitation   ======

Example 1: Mr. Whipples, living in a community-property state, dies after January 1, 1977, with a gross estate of $460,000, with $30,000 of allowable Sections 2053 and 2054 expenses (all applicable to the community-property). Even though this decedent has no separate property, there is a $50,000 marital deduction, calculated as follows:

1. 50% of AGE limitation $ zero
   (no separate property)
2. $250,000 limitation:
   (a) Maximum $250,000
   (b) Less community-property
       adjustment:
       (i) Community-property
           in gross estate $230,000
       (ii) Sections 2053 and
            2054 expenses
            deducted   −30,000*
   (c) Community-property
       adjustment $200,000
   (d) Resulting limitation $ 50,000

* Separate property × $30,000 = $0 per Section 2056(c)(2)(B)(iv).
Then, under Section 2056(c)(1)(c)(ii), $30,000 less $0 = $30,000.

Notice, as Example 1 illustrates, that it is now possible for a decedent to receive a marital deduction even though there is no separate property.

Gift Deductions

A second reduction is required under Section 2056(c)(1)(B) when the decedent has made gifts after December 31, 1976, and has claimed a total gift tax marital deduction in excess of 50 percent of the gift tax marital deduction. This situation occurs where the decedent's gifts to his/her spouse total less than $200,000. Here, the $250,000 limitation must be reduced by an amount of the total gift tax marital deduction allowed to the decedent for gifts made after 1976 if it exceeds the total gift tax marital deduction that would have been allowable under the prior 50 percent limitation of the value of such gifts.

Example 2: Decedent had made $160,000 of gifts after 1976 to his/her spouse and had claimed a gift tax marital deduction of $100,000. Thus, the $250,000 estate tax marital deduction must be reduced to $230,000 [$250,000 − ($100,000 − $80,000)].

An *increase* in the estate tax marital deduction may occur where there is a generation-skipping tax. If a generation-skipping transfer occurs at the same time as (or within nine months after) the death of the deemed transferor, then for purposes of the estate tax marital deduction, the value of the gross estate of the transferor is deemed to be increased by the amount of such transfer under Section 2602(c)(5).

Income Splitting

The marital deduction originated with the Revenue Act of 1948, which also allowed the income splitting advantages of filing joint returns. The purpose of the marital deduction is to eliminate the tax advantages held by those persons domiciled in community-property states.* These statutes provided all taxpayers the same tax treatment that was theoretically and actually possible in community-property states. Thus, for tax purposes, Congress made the community-property system applicable to all the states.

For estate tax purposes, a marital deduction is allowed for the value of all property passing outright to the surviving spouse. This deduction is limited to 50 percent of the value of the adjusted gross

* Arizona, California, Idaho, Louisiana, Nevada, New Mexico, Texas, and Washington.

estate unless this amount is less than $250,000, in which case the previously mentioned adjustments must be considered. The adjusted gross estate is found by subtracting from the entire value of the gross estate the community-property and the adjusted amount of the deductions allowed for funeral expenses, administrative expenses, debts of the decedents, and casualty and theft losses (that is, Sections 2053 and 2054 expenses).[6]

Shared Property Interests

Transfers that qualify for the marital deduction include property interests taken by the surviving spouse under the will, under the laws of intestacy, by rights of survivorship by the entirety or as joint tenants, as a beneficiary of life insurance, and other interests. Normally, in order to qualify for the marital deduction, the property must pass outright.

Terminable Interest

If the surviving spouse receives a *terminable* interest in the property, it does not qualify for the marital deduction. A terminable interest is interest that will terminate or fail after a certain period of time, or upon the happening of some contingency, or upon the failure of some event to occur.[7] For example, a "naked life estate" to a spouse is a terminable interest. Section 2056(d)(3) lists a number of items that qualify as passing to the surviving spouse:

1. The interest is bequeathed or devised to the spouse.
2. The interest is inherited by the spouse.

3. Such interest is the dower or curtesy interest (or statutory interest in lieu thereof) of such person as surviving spouse of the decedent.
4. Such interest has been transferred to the spouse by the decedent at any time (that is, gift is in contemplation of death).
5. Property held in joint ownership with right of survivorship.
6. Power to appoint such interest and has appointed such interest.
7. Proceeds of life insurance received by the surviving spouse.

Example 3: Husband dies, leaving his entire estate to a trust, with income to be paid to his wife for life and the remainder to his children. The transfer to the trust does not qualify for a marital deduction because it is a terminable interest under Section 2056(b).

Example 4: Husband sold property to one son, subject to his continuous use of the property for 15 years, for $30,000 (the fair market value of the remainder interest transferred to the son). When husband died, he still had the right to use the property for eight more years; he left this right to his wife. Since Section 2056(b)(1)(A) is not met, this transfer qualifies for the marital deduction. Assume that, instead of selling the property to the son, husband had given the property to him. Section 2056(b)(1)(A) would be met and the transfer would not qualify for the marital deduction.

Three exceptions to the terminable interest rule apply to property passing to the surviving spouse that would otherwise be considered a terminable interest and would be nondeductible. The three exceptions that may still qualify for the marital deduction are:

1. Property passing to the surviving spouse with the only condition being that he/she survive by a period not to exceed six months, and in fact that he/she does survive the decedent by such a period.[8]

2. Property passing from the decedent either in trust or as a legal life estate where the surviving spouse has a general power of appointment and is entitled to all income from such property. This income must be paid to the survivor at least annually.[9]

Example 5: A decedent's will provides for the creation of a marital trust, with income to be distributed at least quarterly to the surviving spouse. At the death of the surviving spouse, trust income is to be accumulated and added to principal for a period of two years, after which the trust terminates and all assets are to be paid to such individuals as the spouse has designated by will. This testamentary general power of appointment could be exercised in favor of the surviving spouse's estate.

The corpus of the trust would be included in the surviving spouse's estate because there was a general power of appointment. But in Rev. Rul. 76-502, IRB 1976-51, 15, the IRS indicated that this testamentary power did not conform to Reg. 20.2056(b)-5(g)(2) and a marital deduction was not allowed. Thus, the continuation of a trust beyond the death of a powerholder that was not completely attributable to a default of exercise or temporary administrative difficulties will result in a denial of the marital deduction.

Example 6: A decedent bequeathed to her husband an income interest in her property for life, payable annually, and a lifetime power of invasion exercisable on the surviving spouse's behalf in all events. A fee simple absolute interest in the property is not necessary for a marital deduction. Thus, this interest in property qualifies for the marital deduction under Section 2056(d)(5).

3. Life insurance or annuity payments held by the insurer with a general power of appointment held by the surviving spouse. If the proceeds are payable in installments, the installments or interest must be paid to the surviving spouse at least annually.[10]

Formula Bequests

In order to secure the maximum marital deduction, many wills contain a formula bequest expressed in terms of 50 percent of the adjusted gross estate or the maximum allowable marital deduction. The exact form of a marital bequest clause can have important consequences on the property distributed to the beneficiaries of the decedent; thus, careful consideration must be given to the drafting of such a clause. To take advantage of the new $250,000 deduction, most wills must be modified or executed after December 31, 1976.

Orphan's Exclusion

The last parent dying after 1976 is allowed an orphan's exclusion for transfers to minor children with no known surviving parent. A "minor child" is any child of the decedent (including adopted children) who is less than 21 years of age at the decedent's death. The amount of the exclusion per child is limited to $5,000 multiplied by the number by which 21 exceeds the child's age in years on the date of the parent's death. "An adoption in contemplation of death" should *not* be a valid tax technique, since the House of Representatives has indicated that "an adoption will not supplant the relationship of blood where it can be shown that the adoption was motivated to obtain the benefits of this provision." [11] Also, under Section 2056(b), no deduction is allowed for a life estate interest or terminable interest passing to the child. But an interest is not terminable solely because the property will pass to another individual if the child dies before the youngest child of the decedent attains the age of 21.

Example 7: Mr. Engulf, a widower, dies after 1976, survived by his daughter, age 15. The decedent is allowed an orphan's exclusion of $30,000 [$5,000 × (21 − 15)], assuming at least this amount is passed to the daughter.

COMPUTATION OF TAX

To determine the tax base, the taxable estate must be increased by the adjusted taxable gifts made after December 31, 1976. The adjusted taxable gifts are simply the sum of all taxable gifts made after December 31, 1976, and before three years prior to the decedent's death. One point of caution is necessary here: The gross amount of gifts is less all deductions such as the annual exclusions and the marital deduction.

Gross Estate Tax

The gross estate tax is computed by using the new unified rate schedule found in Section 2001. These new rates, which apply to citizens and residents of the United States, range from 18 percent on the first $10,000 to 70 percent on the entire taxable estate in excess of $5,000,000.[12] The tax computed at these rates, however, is subject to reduction by various credits allowed on account of other taxes. Some of the credits allowed as deductions from the gross estate tax payable when calculating the net estate tax payable are state death tax credit, a credit for tax on prior transfers, credit for foreign death taxes, and the new unified estate and gift tax credit. These credits are discussed below. (The unified rate schedule can be found in Appendix B at the end of this book.)

Credits Allowable

A credit is allowed against the federal estate tax for the amount of any estate, inheritance, legacy, or succession taxes actually paid to any state, territory, or the District of Columbia with respect to any property included in the decedent's gross estate. If the decedent's taxable estate does not exceed $40,000, there is no credit allowed for state death taxes. If the taxable estate exceeds $40,000, the credit is limited by an amount determined by the table in Section 2011(b).

Example 8:   Decedent's taxable estate is $300,000 and his executor paid $3,800 state estate taxes. The taxable estate is reduced by $60,000 before looking for the maximum credit for state death taxes in the table in Section 2011(b). The maximum allowable credit is $3,600.

The credit for state death taxes is limited to those taxes that were actually paid. Basically, the credit must be claimed within four years after the filing of the estate tax return for the decedent's estate.

Since a credit is allowed only up to the amount of state taxes paid, care should be taken to supply the required information in full. This is particularly important when a deposit is made with the state as security for the payment of the state tax. It is also important when discounts or refunds may be allowed by the state. The information to be furnished to the district director should disclose the total amount of tax imposed by the state, the amount of any discount allowed, the total amount actually paid in cash, and the identity of the property for which the state tax has been paid or is to be paid.[13]

Post-Mortem Planning

Post-mortem estate planning is possible with state death taxes. Instead of claiming state death taxes (imposed on a transfer for public, charitable, or religious uses) as a credit, an executor may elect to deduct these expenditures. The conditions for making this election are outlined in Reg. 20.2053-9(b).

For all or a part of the estate tax paid with respect to the transfer of property to the decedent by someone who died within ten years before or within two years after the decedent's death, a credit is allowed against the estate tax. The credit for tax on prior transfers is allowed only for prior estate taxes, not gift taxes. Also, within limits, it is allowed for more than two successive decedents. If the transferor died within two years before or after the present decedent's death, the credit allowed for the tax is 100 percent of the maximum amount allowable. If the transferor predeceased the decedent by more than two years, the credit allowable is reduced by 20 percent for each full two years by which the death of the transferor preceded that of the present decedent.[14]

The credit for tax on prior transfers is limited to the smaller of the following amounts:

1. An amount that bears the same ratio to the transferor's adjusted federal estate tax as the value of the transferred property bears to the transferor's adjusted taxable estate.

2. The amount by which the estate tax of the present decedent as determined without regard to a credit on prior transfers exceeds the estate tax for his/her estate as determined by excluding from the gross estate the net value of the transfer.[15]

Since many other countries levy death taxes on the transfer by nonresident aliens of property situated within their boundaries, the estates of many United States citizens are subjected to double taxes. Thus, our federal government has entered into estate tax conventions with a number of foreign countries to provide relief from such double taxation.

To protect against double taxation, the estate is allowed a credit against the federal estate tax for any inheritance, estate, legacy, or succession tax paid to a foreign country and its political subdivisions on any property that is included in the decedent's gross estate. The credit for foreign death taxes is limited to the smaller of the following amounts: the amount of the foreign death tax attributable to such property situated in the country imposing the tax and included in the decedent's gross estate; or the amount of the federal estate taxes attributable to such property.[16]

For the credit to be allowed, the taxpayer must establish to the satisfaction of the Secretary of State the amount of taxes actually paid to the foreign country, the amount and date of each payment, and the description and value of the property with respect to which taxes were imposed. He may also have to submit other information necessary for the verification and computation of the credit.

Gift Tax Paid

To be allowed, this credit must be claimed within four years after the filing of the estate tax return.[17] Since under the new law, taxable gifts made after December 31, 1976, become part of the tax base and thus subject to the tax rate, any gift tax rate paid on gifts made after December 31, 1976, may be subtracted from the gross estate tax. Thus, in essence, the tax paid on such gifts becomes a credit against the estate tax.

An executor may elect to deduct certain foreign death taxes (imposed on a transfer for public, charitable, or religious uses) rather than claiming such taxes as a tax credit. The conditions to be met in order to make this election are outlined in Reg. 20.2053-10(b).

Unified Estate and Gift Tax Credit

The Tax Reform Act of 1976 created a new unified estate and gift tax credit which in effect replaces the old estate tax exemption of $60,000 and the gift tax exemption of $30,000. This new unified credit is being phased in over five years, beginning as a credit of $30,000 in 1977 and increasing to a credit of $47,000 in 1981 and thereafter.

Year of Death	Amount of Credit	Amount of Equivalent Exemption
1977	$30,000	$120,667
1978	34,000	134,000
1979	38,000	147,333
1980	42,500	161,563
1981	47,000	175,625

The equivalent exemption is the amount of the taxable estate that passes free of the unified estate tax at death.

This credit (like the other credits) is deducted directly from the gross estate tax to determine the net estate tax payable. The net estate tax payable is the amount that becomes due to the Internal Revenue Service within nine months after the death unless an extension of time is granted.[18]

The mechanical calculation of the estate tax can best be summarized by observing the simplified format developed by Barry R. Schimel, as shown on pages 74–75.

ESTATE-PLANNING TIPS

The federal estate tax laws are quite complicated and involved. Therefore, an estate planner must have a firm understanding of these laws and be aware of their interrelationships with the income tax laws. The estate owner must consider the impact of the estate tax in his estate planning. The estate owner's objectives should be to maximize the use of his assets in the way he thinks best. However, some helpful hints to enable the estate owner to minimize his taxes may be outlined as follows:

1. The estate owner should keep accurate inventories of assets and investments. He/she should make certain that another person knows the location of his/her will assets and inventory assets.

2. A taxable estate should not be closed in less than six months after the date of the decedent's death. Only then can an administrator determine whether the alternate valuation date should be elected.

3. An excellent way to reduce an individual's estate tax liability is to reduce the gross estate by a systematic program of lifetime giving. Succeeding subsections discuss ways in which a portion of an estate can be transferred without incurring a gift tax.

4. Generally, the advantage of a fresh-start step-up-basis to the estate and heirs of a decedent indicates that an individual should try to retain until death any noncash property that has substantially appreciated in value before 1977. Although such a procedure maximizes the estate tax, it eliminates any income tax that would have resulted if the property had been sold before death.

5. There may be savings in administrative costs and taxes if certain assets are sold immediately prior to death. Such "sales in contemplation of death" remove the capital gains tax paid on the sales from the gross estate. The capital gains tax does not have to be "grossed up" as does the tax on deathbed gifts.

Simplified Format to Estimate the Estate Tax under the 1976 Tax Reform Act

Total assets of estate	$ _____
Gifts during last three years (1)	+ _____
Gross estate	$ _____
Less: liabilities of estate	− _____
expenses (2)	− _____
Adjusted gross estate	$ _____
Less: marital deduction (3)	
or	
orphan's exclusion (4)	− _____
Less: charitable deduction	− _____
Taxable estate	$ _____
Gifts made after 1976 (5)	+ _____
Tentative taxable base	$ _____
Estate tax from unified rate	
schedule	$ _____
Less: gift taxes previously	
paid (6)	− _____
Unified tax credit (7)	− _____
Net estate tax payable	$ _____

Numbers in parentheses refer to notes on opposite page.

This technique may be beneficial, since the tax add-on-to-basis does *not* include the amount of the transfer tax applicable to any carry-over basis.

6. At least $250,000 should be left to the spouse, since the marital deduction after 1976 is the greater of two amounts: $250,000 or one-half of the dece-

---

NOTES

(1) If post-1976 gifts are made within three years of death, the full amount of the gifts, including the amount of gift taxes paid, less the $3,000 annual exclusions, are includable in the gross estate.

(2) Funeral and medical expenses estimate $4,500–$5,000. Administrative expenses estimate 3% of the gross estate or 5% of the probate estate.

(3) The actual amount passing to the surviving spouse not to exceed $250,000 or 50% of the adjusted gross estate, whichever is greater.

(4) This exclusion is available only if there is no surviving spouse nor surviving parent of the child (such as in the case of a divorce). Every year each child is under age 21 is multiplied by $5,000, provided this amount of taxable estate actually passes to the child.

(5) Taxable gifts made after 1976, with the exception of gifts within three years of death (see item 1 above). The taxable gift is the amount of the gift minus the marital deduction and the $3,000 annual exclusion.

(6) Gift taxes actually paid on gifts after 1976, including gifts in items 1 and 5 above.

(7) Varies depending on year of death:
1977 = $30,000
1978 = $34,000
1979 = $38,000
1980 = $42,000
1981 and after = $47,000
Gifts made from September 9, 1976, to December 31, 1976, will reduce the unified credit by 20% of the portion of the previous lifetime exclusion used.

Source: B. R. Schimel, "Estimating the Estate Under the 1976 Reform Act," *Journal of Accountancy*, July 1977, p. 42. Reprinted with permission. © 1977 by the American Institute of Certified Public Accountants, Inc.

dent's adjusted gross estate. By leaving approximately 50 percent of the adjusted gross estate (in a large estate) to the surviving spouse, the decedent spouse can obtain the maximum marital deduction. However, since the marital deduction is limited to 50 percent of AGE in a large estate, there are no tax benefits in giving the spouse much more than 50 percent. Anything above the 50 percent level will be taxed twice: in the decedent's estate and again in the surviving spouse's estate. Of course, where both estates are large, a marital deduction may not be advisable, since the appropriate objective is to minimize the taxes on the estates of *both* spouses. This objective may call for no property to be transferred to the surviving spouse.

7. In order to get the marital deduction, there must be a surviving spouse. If there is a common disaster, the law presumes that each survived the other. Therefore, neither will inherit from the other and there will be no marital deduction. If one of the estates is much larger than the other, a provision should be placed in the will stating that the beneficiary survived the spouse with the larger estate. However, with the larger marital deduction, it may be better to include *some* of the assets in the wife's estate in order to qualify for the estate tax marital deduction. Some simple language in the will should accomplish this objective.

8. To a limited extent a decedent can bypass or "skip" a generation. For example, a father can pass to his son (or daughter) only the right to receive income from certain assets, with the remainder to go to his grandchildren. There is no tax on

generation-skipping transfers to grandchildren up to $250,000 per grandchild on the date of the termination of the grantor-children life income interest. Thus, to a limited extent, the assets are not included in the child's estate and the estate tax is avoided. For example, if a grantor has three children (who also have children), up to $750,000 can be transferred to the grandchildren tax-free.

9. A husband should consider giving up all "incidents of ownership" in insurance policies. If his wife owns all the insurance policies covering his life, none of the policies will be included in his gross estate. The husband should also own the policies on his wife's life. Remember, only the *value of the policy on the date of the gift* is included in "taxable gifts." Of course, this assignment is not for everyone (that is, the marriage may be unstable). Also, if the spouse has very little experience in managing money, some type of trust arrangement may be appropriate.

For example, a life insurance trust may be established with all incidents of ownership of the insurance policy. The trust would collect the insurance proceeds, and the trustee would have certain discretionary powers, such as lending money to the estate. Or the trustee could be empowered to use the trust income for the widow and/or children.

10. Where there is a chance that a donor will die before the donee reaches 21 years of age, the donor should *not* be the custodian of a transfer under the Uniform Gifts to Minors Act. If the donor is the custodian and dies, the value of the custodian property will be included in his estate.

11. The new law has reduced the value of one tax-planning technique—flower bonds. Flower bonds are certain treasury bonds that bear a low interest rate and may be bought at a discount, but are redeemable at par in payment of a decedent's federal estate tax. However, the bonds must be included in the estate at face value. Before the changes introduced by the law, the excess of the face value of the bonds above their purchase price escaped the *income* tax because the tax basis of the bonds was stepped up to their face value on date of death. This excess is now taxable when the executor uses the bonds to pay the federal estate tax.

12. Flower bonds are advantageous in a community-property state, for they may be used *to create a marital deduction.* Here is how this technique can be used. Phillips' one-half of community property is worth $4.8 million. Immediately before his death, he borrowed $1 million on his separate credit in order to purchase flower bonds with a par value of $1.2 million. His gross estate is now $6 million:

$4.8	community-property
1.2	separate property
$6.0	gross estate

Assume that decedent's administrative expenses are $200,000. Adjusted gross estate (AGE) must be calculated in order to determine the maximum marital deduction. But only an allocable portion of the Sections 2053 and 2054 items are deductible in arriving at AGE, or $240,000. The marital deduction would be calculated as follows:

$6,000,000	gross estate
(4,800,000)	community-property
(240,000)	allocable administrative expense
$ 960,000	
× 0.50	
$ 480,000	marital deduction

Thus, a $480,000 marital deduction is created in a community-property state by the judicious use of flower bonds to create "instant separate property."

13. Mention should be made of the fact that the new rules involving the community-property adjustment create an unusual situation. For small- and medium-sized community-property estates ($500,000 or less), a marital deduction may be available *even though there may be no separate property.*

14. When satisfying charitable bequests, the executor may wish to distribute property with the lowest carry-over basis to charitable organizations. Such a procedure allows the executor to distribute the higher-basis property to the family of the decedent.

15. Before revising a will that was in existence on April 30, 1976, consideration must be given to the fact that any revision may cause the will or trust to fall within the new generation-skipping tax area.

REFERENCES

1. Section 2053; Reg. 20.2053-2.
2. Section 2053; Reg. 20.2053-3.
3. Section 2053; Reg. 20.2053-6, 20.2053-7.
4. Reg. 20.2053-1(d); Reg. 1.642(g)(1).

5. Section 2055.
6. Section 2056.
7. Section 2056(b).
8. Section 2056(b)-3.
9. Section 2056(b)-5.
10. Section 2056(b)-6.
11. H. Rep. 94-1380, 94th Cong., 2d Sess. 60 (1976).
12. Section 2001.
13. Reg. 20.2011-1(b)(2).
14. Section 2013.
15. Reg. 20-2013-2 and 20-2013-3.
16. Section 2014.
17. Section 2014(d)(e).
18. Sections 6075 and 6151.

5

Deferral
and Financing
of the Estate Tax
Liability

The mere fact that a taxpayer chooses one road
in preference to another, in order to
avoid the hot sun of taxation, is no reason to deny
he actually traveled the first road.
Hugh C. Bickford

AN estate tax return (Form 706) is due within nine
months of a decedent's death. The District Director's office is authorized to extend the time for filing
up to six months upon written request and a show-
ing of reasonable cause. Some situations that may

be recognized as reasonable cause are pending litigation, illness of the executor or attorney, or circumstances that make it impossible to determine the nature or extent of an asset. Except in the case of a taxpayer who is abroad, the extension *cannot* be for more than six months. Receiving an extension does prevent a delinquency penalty from being assessed, but interest accrues under Section 6621(a) during the extension at 9 percent per year. If no extension is obtained, 9 percent interest is charged on the amount of tax not paid by the due date; likewise, there is a nondeductible 0.5 percent penalty tax due per month up to a maximum of 25 percent (Section 6651).

PAYMENT OF TAX LIABILITY

The tax liability must be sent to the District Director's office with the return, unless the estate qualifies for special treatment under one of the provisions that allows an extension of time for payment. The extensions apply to reasonable cause, reversionary or remainder interests, and large interests in closely held corporations. If payment cannot be made with the return, due to reasonable cause such as being forced to liquidate assets in a depressed market, the District Director's office may extend the time for submitting the payment. The extension can be granted .for a period ranging from one year to a maximum of ten years. As is true with all extensions, interest accrues from the due date of the return. Prior to December 31, 1976, exceptional circumstances had to be shown in order to receive this extension. The Tax Reform Act of 1976 substituted the phrase "reasonable cause" for "undue hardship" in this provision. If a farm or closely held business constitutes at least 35 percent of the adjusted gross estate, then "reasonable cause" is presumed to exist.

If an estate includes a reversionary or remainder interest, an extension of time for payment may be elected by the executor under Section 6163. The tax attributable to the value of the interest may be postponed up to six months after the termination of the decedent's interest in the property. If at this time payment would result in undue hardship (as discussed above), the District office may postpone the payment date for a reasonable period, up to a maximum of three years. Since the extension applies only to the tax on the reversionary or remainder interest, the portion of the tax attributable to the other assets must be submitted with the estate tax return.

The two extensions discussed above must be requested in writing on or before the due date of the tax return. The reasonable-cause extension is discretionary with the District office, but the postponement for reversionary or business interests may be elected by the estate if the requirements are met. Extensions of time for payment are usually applied for simultaneously with the filing of the return. Both extensions are available to postpone the payment of any deficiency that may arise from a subsequent audit of the return, provided the requirements are met at that time.

DEFERMENTS AND EXTENSIONS

Closely Held Business Extension: Section 6166A

A third extension that may be elected is provided by statute in order to relieve any hardship imposed on estates that consist largely of closely held businesses. This extension is intended to prevent a forced liquidation to pay the tax when it is due with the return. The postponement applies only to the amount of tax attributable to the inclusion of the business in the estate. Any tax generated by other assets must be paid when the return is due. Extended payments may be made yearly for up to ten years.

Several qualifications must be met in order to obtain the advantage of this extension. The most important of these is the requirement that the value of the business interest exceed 35 percent of the gross estate or 50 percent of the taxable estate. As is necessarily true with any of the extensions, there are also limitations on the amount of tax that can be postponed. All the qualifications and limitations are enumerated at Section 6166A.

Fifteen-Year Installment Provision: Section 6166

Effective after December 31, 1976, there is a fifteen-year installment provision for qualifying interest in a farm or other closely held business. An executor may *defer all payments* of tax for *five* years and pay only interest for such period. For years 6 through 15 after the decedent's death, the tax is payable in equal installments. A low 4 percent interest rate applies to the estate tax on the first $1 million in value of a farm or closely held business. In order to qualify, the interest in the closely held business (proprietor, partner, and stockholder) or farm must exceed 65 percent of the decedent's adjusted gross estate (AGE). AGE refers to gross estate less expenses, debts, claims, and losses, but before marital and charitable deductions. In order to qualify, it may be worthwhile to give securities or other property to heir(s) before death in order to make sure that the required proportion of the estate consists of farm or business property. Further, a taxpayer may wish to delay giving children a share of the farm or family business before he dies.

The payment of the estate tax is accelerated if one-third or more of a decedent's qualifying interest is disposed of, or if there is a withdrawal of money (or other property) in an amount equal to one-third of the value of the decedent's interest (a Section 303 redemption is excepted).

Where an election is made to pay taxes in installments under Section 6166 or Section 6166A, a special lien procedure may be elected so that an executor will not be personally liable for the taxes. The executor and all beneficiaries with an interest in the qualifying property must file a written agreement, consenting to the creation of a lien, and designate a responsible person to deal with the IRS as an agent for the appropriate parties.

Redemption under Section 303

Owners of corporations should not overlook a Section 303 redemption that provides an opportunity to take assets out of a family corporation at a favorable sale or exchange treatment (that is, capital gain provisions). Under this provision an estate or the heirs of the stockholder of a corporation may withdraw cash or property from the enterprise without paying a dividend tax, provided the amount is equal to the sum of federal and estate death taxes and funeral and administrative expenses. Further, the gain may be reduced on such a redemption, since the stock may have received a fresh-start step-up-in-basis under Section 1023(h). The purpose of this special redemption is to *help the financing of the estate taxes* in situations where the estate consists mainly of shares of stock in a closely held corporation.

An option can be created to give the administrator for the decedent's estate the right to require the corporation to redeem from the estate an amount of stock that will provide the necessary liquid assets to pay death taxes, and funeral and administrative expenses under Section 303. Such an option can be placed in a written agreement between the stockholder and the corporation, and should be so designed as to meet the requirements of Section 303.

REQUIREMENTS AND LIMITATIONS

A number of requirements and limitations must be satisfied in order to obtain capital gain treatment under Section 303.

1. There must be a distribution of property to a stockholder by a corporation in redemption of all or part of the stock of such corporation.

2. Such stock must be included in determining

the gross estate of a decedent for purposes of the federal estate tax.

3. The value of the stock included in the decedent's estate must be more than 50 percent of the adjusted gross estate after 1976.[1]

4. The amount treated as a capital gain can be no greater than the sum of the death taxes and the funeral and administrative expenses allowable under Sections 2053 or 2106.

5. Qualifying redemptions are limited to those post-1976 stockholders whose interest in the estate is reduced directly (or through a binding obligation to contribute) by any payment of death taxes or funeral and administrative expenses.

6. Any distribution made more than four years after the decedent's death is subject to additional limitations.[2]

Inclusion in an Estate

The redeemed stock must be included in the gross estate of a decedent for federal estate tax purposes.[3] Such included stock must have a federal estate tax value more than 50 percent of the value of the adjusted gross estate. Adjusted gross estate (AGE) is defined as gross estate less the sum of the deductions *allowable* under Sections 2053 or 2054.[4] These allowable deductions include: [5]

1. Funeral expenses.
2. Administrative expenses.
3. Claims against the estate.
4. Unpaid mortgages and other indebtedness.
5. Losses incurred by the estate.

Note that the term "allowable" (rather than "allowed") will permit an executor to claim administrative expenses as *income* tax deductions without adversely affecting qualification under the 50 percent test.[6]

A special rule applies to an estate that includes stock of two or more corporations. If neither block of stock satisfies the 50 percent requirement, this special rule permits treatment of the combined holdings as stock in a single corporation. To qualify, however, the estate tax value of the stock held in each corporation must be more than 75 percent in value of the outstanding stock of such corporation. For purposes of this 75 percent test, the surviving spouse's community-property interest in such stock is treated as if it were included in the decedent's gross estate.[7]

Example 1: The gross estate of a decedent, Pete Rose, has a fair market value of $1 million, and the Sections 2053 and 2054 expenses are $125,000. Included in the gross estate are stocks in three corporations:

	Adjusted Basis	Fair Market Value
Bay	$110,000	$200,000
Melk	125,000	400,000
Whip	75,000	200,000

The stock of Bay and Melk included in the estate is *all* the outstanding stock of the two corporations. Neither of the stockholdings satisfies the 50 percent of adjusted-gross-estate test. However, since Bay and Melk meet the 75 percent test, the stock of both corporations can be treated as stock of a single corporation valued at $600,000. Clearly, $600,000 is greater than 50 percent of AGE [50 × ($1 million − $125,000) = $437,500].

The 50 percent test is critical to the use of a Section 303 redemption. If the stockholdings do not satisfy this test, certain steps may be taken to insure qualification. The value of a stockholder's interest in a corporation may be increased, the stockholder's adjusted gross estate may be decreased, or a combination of both can be employed in order to qualify for Section 303 treatment. For example, a stockholder could purchase more shares in the corporation. Further, assets other than closely held stock may be given away more than three years before death in order to help satisfy the 50 percent test.[8]

There is one exception to the requirement that the stock must be included in the gross estate. Section 303(c) provides exchange treatment to a redemption of stock possessing a substituted basis acquired from stock that was included in the gross estate. For example, stock may have been included in the decedent's gross estate and later exchanged for other stock in a nontaxable reorganization. The latter stock can qualify under Section 303.

Limitation of Amount

Even if an estate has sufficient liquid assets in order to pay its taxes and expenses without a redemption, qualified stockholders can still obtain the benefits of Section 303. In fact, Section 303 is applicable even though the proceeds are not used to pay federal estate taxes or even when there is no federal estate tax due.[9] However, the amount of the redemption is limited to the total of the death taxes and the funeral and administrative expenses of the estate.[10]

When there is more than one redemption distribution during the prescribed time period, the distribution is applied against the total amount that qualifies for exchange treatment, in the order in which the distributions were made. All distributions are considered, including distributions that fall under a different Code provision.[11]

Example 2: Decedent's gross estate is $800,000 and the sum of death taxes and funeral and administrative expenses is $225,000. Included in determining gross estate is stock of a corporation that is valued at $450,000 for estate tax purposes. In the first year of administration, one-third of the stock is distributed to a legatee, and shortly thereafter the corporation redeems it for $150,000. In the second year, another one-third of the stock includable in the estate is redeemed for $150,000. The first distribution is applied against the $225,000 that qualifies for Section 303 treatment as payment in exchange for stock under Section 302(a). On the second distribution, only $75,000 is treated as in-full payment in exchange for stock under Section 303.

Time Limitation

This special time limitation treatment applies only to distributions made in redemption of such stock in either of two situations:

1. The period between the decedent's death and the ninetieth day after the expiration of the limitation period in Section 6501(a) (that is, three years). Since the federal estate tax return is due nine months after the decedent's death under Section

6075(a), the qualified limitation is approximately four years.

2. In the case of Tax Court litigation, the permissible time period is extended for 60 days after the Tax Court's decision becomes final.[12]

If an election is made under Sections 6166 or 6166A, relating to the extension of time to pay the estate tax attributable to a farm or closely held business, the Section 303 period is identical with these extension periods.[13] However, any amounts distributed after the four-year period are still limited to the sum of the death taxes and funeral and administrative expenses.[14]

Qualifying Stockholders

For estates of decedents dying before 1977, Section 303 was not limited to redemptions from stockholders liable for the payment of death taxes or other expenses. In fact, such a redemption applied to redeemed stock held by an individual who, as a result of survival, owned the stock before or immediately after the decedent's death. Pre-1977 qualifying stockholders include an executor, heir, a surviving joint tenant, a surviving spouse, a donee of a gift in contemplation of death, an appointee, a trustee of a trust created by the decedent, or a taker in default of appointment.

However, the regulations did not extend exchange treatment to subsequent purchasers or donees,[15] but the Fifth Circuit Court did extend Section 303 treatment to a person who used the redemption proceeds to pay expenditures of the decedent's estate.[16]

For estates of decedents dying after 1976, a qualifying redemption is limited to those stockholders whose interest in the estate is reduced (directly or through a binding obligation to contribute) by the payment of the death taxes and funeral and administration expenses, and to the extent of such reduction.[17] Thus, items such as property qualifying for the marital deduction will *no longer* be eligible for Section 303 treatment.

New special rules apply to generation-skipping transfers. Where stock in a corporation is subject to a generation-skipping tax, such stock will be included in the gross estate of the deemed transferor. Any tax imposed under Section 2601 will be treated as an estate tax, thereby increasing the amount available for Section 303 treatment. The period of distribution is measured from the date of the generation-skipping transfer, and the relationship of the stock to the decedent's estate is measured with reference solely to the amount of the generation-skipping transfer.[18]

New Carry-over Basis

Section 303 redemptions are affected adversely by the new carry-over basis rules. For years after 1976 there is generally a carry-over basis.[19] Property will no longer receive a stepped-up basis. However, the basis of property acquired from a decedent dying after December 31, 1976, may be stepped up, in general, only to the extent of any appreciation *before* 1977. Marketable bonds and securities are stepped up to their fair market value as of December 31, 1976.[20] The amount of the appreciation occurring in property prior to 1977, other than marketable bonds and securities, is determined by a ratio multiplied by the total amount of appreciation occurring over the entire period during which a taxpayer is treated as holding the asset. This ratio is calculated by dividing the number of days that the asset has been held by the decedent before 1977 by the total number of days that the taxpayer held the property.[21]

Thus, most of the stock being redeemed will have appreciated in value, and the redemption will produce capital gains, subject to taxation. Of course subsequent redemption, in order to raise funds to pay such income taxes, is not protected by Section 303.

Example 3:   Decedent's gross estate is $1 million, and the Sections 2053 and 2054 expenses are $225,000. Included in determining gross estate is stock of a corporation that is valued at $450,000 for estate tax purposes [adjusted basis of $150,000 and a Section 1023(h) basis of $240,000]. In the first year of administration, one-third of the stock is distributed to a legatee, and shortly thereafter the corporation redeems it for $150,000. In the second year, another one-third of the stock includable in the estate is redeemed for $160,000. During the first year, the entire distribution would qualify for exchange treatment. Thus, a $70,000 capital gain would be recognized ($150,000 − $80,000) for the first year. As for the second year, only $75,000 of the distribution may be protected by Section 303. Thus, there would be a $37,500 capital gain [$75,000 − ($75,000/160,000 × $80,000)]. The remaining $150,000 distribution must qualify under a "safe harbor" in Section 302; otherwise the $150,000 would be treated as a dividend.

REFERENCES

1. Section 303. Before 1977, the stock so included must have had a federal estate tax value of either (1) more than 35 percent of the gross estate, or (2) 50 percent of the taxable estate.
2. See Section 203(b).
3. Section 303(a).
4. Section 303(b)(2)(A).
5. Sections 2053 and 2054.
6. Rev. Rul. 56-449, 1956-2 C.B. 180.
7. Section 303(b)(2)(B).
8. See also Chan, "Planning a Sec. 303 Redemption," *The Tax Adviser*, January 1976, p. 7.
9. Section 303(a).
10. Rev. Rul. 56-60, 1956-1 C.B. 443.
11. Reg. 1.303-2(g)(1).
12. Section 303(b)(1)(A) and (B).
13. Section 303(b)(1)(C).
14. Section 303(b)(4).
15. Reg. 1.303-2(f).
16. *Nancy Lake* v. *Commissioner*, 406 F. 2d 941 (5th Cir. 1969).
17. Section 303(b)(3).
18. Section 303(d).
19. Section 1023(a)(1).
20. Section 1023(h)(2).
21. Section 1023(h)(1).

6

Lifetime Gifts

**Estate planning is the process of passing from
this world into the next without passing
through the Internal Revenue Service.**
Robert Brosterman

THE federal gift tax is a tax levied upon transfer of
gifts from one person (donor) to another person
(donee). The difference between a gift and inheritance is that a gift is the transmission of property
from one living person to another. To further qualify
as a gift, property must be given without any consideration.

The federal gift tax originated in the Revenue
Act of 1932. Its primary purpose was to act as a
backstop to the federal estate tax; it was not intended to raise revenues. The establishment of the

gift tax prevented people from avoiding the progressive federal estate tax by distributing assets during their lifetime. An interesting note is that, although the yield of this tax and the dollar value of gifts are relatively small, lifetime giving is almost universal in the higher wealth categories.

Before 1977 the gift tax rates were 25 percent less than federal estate tax rates, and a systematic pattern of lifetime giving could reduce significantly an individual's federal estate tax liability as well as his income tax payments. This old two-tax rate system was eliminated after December 31, 1976, and a single, progressive transfer tax is now imposed on the cumulative total of both lifetime gifts and property owned at death. The lowest effective rate after considering a unified credit is 18 percent, as compared to the pre-1977 bottom 3 percent rate. The highest rate is 70 percent for cumulative taxable transfers in excess of $5 million. The new unified rates, which are presented in Appendix B at the end of this book, are at least one-third as high as the pre-1977 gift tax rates.

REQUIREMENTS OF A GIFT

The statutes fail to give an exact definition of a gift. As set forth by Section 2511(a), the gift tax applies "whether the transfer is in trust or otherwise, whether the gift is direct or indirect, and whether the property is real or personal, tangible or intangible." Further, Regulation 25.1512-8 states that

> transfers reached by the gift tax are not confined to those only which, being without a valuable consideration, accord with the common law concept of gifts, but

embrace as well sales, exchanges, and other dispositions of property for a consideration to the extent that
the value of the property transferred by the donor exceeds the value in money or money's worth of the consideration given therefor. However, a sale, exchange,
or other transfer of property made in the ordinary
course of business (a transaction which is bona fide, at
arm's length, and free from any donative intent) will be
considered as made for an adequate and full consideration in money or money's worth, as love and affection,
promise of marriage, etc., is to be wholly disregarded,
and the entire value of the property transferred constitutes the amount of the gift. Similarly, a relinquishment or promised relinquishment of dower or curtesy,
or of a statutory estate created in lieu of dower or curtesy, or of other marital rights in the spouse's property
or estate, shall not be considered to any extent a consideration "in money or money's worth."

The Tax Court has stipulated that the six following items are essential elements of a bona fide gift: [1]

1. A donor competent to make a gift;
2. A donee capable of taking the gift;
3. A clear and unmistakable intention on the part of
   the donor to absolutely and irrevocably divest himself of the title, dominion, and control of the subject
   matter of the gift *in praesenti;*
4. There is an actual irrevocable transfer of the present
   legal title and of the dominion and control of the
   entire gift to the donee, so that the donor can exercise no further active dominion or control over it;
5. A delivery to the donee of the subject of the gift or of
   the most effective means of commanding the
   dominion of it; and
6. Acceptance of the gift by the donee.

In viewing items 2 and 6, Regulation 25.2511-2(a)
indicates that, regardless of the fact that the identity

of the donee may not then be known, a gift is considered valid.[2] Also, donative intent on behalf of the donor need not be present in order to incur a gift tax.[3]

PARTIES SUBJECT TO THE TAX AND TIMING OF THE TAX

For all gifts (except qualified charitable transfers) made after 1976, a tax is imposed for each calendar quarter upon the transfers of property by gift from any individuals or by a corporation. A gift tax return does not have to be filed during the year until there is $25,000 of taxable gifts. Both the gift tax return and payment are due on the fifteenth day of the second month following the close of a calendar quarter as follows:

Calendar Quarter	Due Date
March 31, 1978	May 15, 1978
June 30, 1978	August 15, 1978
September 30, 1978	November 15, 1978
December 31, 1978	February 15, 1979

In other words, no quarterly gift tax returns are due until the aggregate taxable gifts exceed $25,000.

Example 1:   Donor makes his first taxable gift of $9,000 to his son on February 12. On June 1 he makes a second taxable gift of $6,000 to his daughter. On September 2, he makes another taxable gift of $7,000 to his wife. Donor would not be required to file a gift tax return until February 15 of the next year.

The important factor is the status of the donor at

the time of the gift and not the location of the gift property. Thus, a transfer of gift property, wherever situated, is taxable (to the extent that value exceeds deductions and exclusions) if the donor is a citizen or resident of the United States. This tax is payable by the donor as stipulated in Section 2502(d). For nonresident aliens, the gift tax is applicable only to the transfer of real and tangible personal property that is located in the United States. Gifts of intangible property made by nonresident aliens for the calendar year 1967 and years thereafter are not subject to gift tax except in the case of certain expatriate U.S. citizens.

PRE-1977 AND POST-1976 EXEMPTIONS, ANNUAL EXCLUSIONS, AND UNIFIED CREDITS

A lifetime specific exemption of $30,000 is allowed for gifts made before 1977 by every citizen and resident in determining his or her net taxable gifts. This exemption could be taken in a single quarter or spread over a number of years in whatever way the donor desires. For years after 1976, the $30,000 lifetime exemption is replaced by the following unified credit:

Year	Amount of Credit	Amount of Equivalent Exemption
1977	$30,000	$120,667
1978	34,000	134,000
1979	38,000	147,333
1980	42,000	161,563
1981	47,000	175,625

Thus, the unified credit is phased in over a five-year period. To the extent any portion of the unified credit is used against lifetime transfers, there is a direct reduction in the amount of the credit available at death.

Furthermore, an annual exclusion of the first $3,000 of gifts of *present* interest to any one donee during the calendar year since 1954 is excluded in determining the taxable gifts of the donor. There is, however, no $3,000 annual exclusion for gifts considered to be *future* interests. So, after 1976, every donor has a single unified credit and an annual exclusion of $3,000 in the determination of taxable gifts.

Gift Splitting

By what is called "gift splitting," a husband and wife could combine their pre-1977 lifetime exemptions for a total of $60,000 and also their annual exclusions, which would total $6,000. For years after 1976, a husband and wife can combine their unified credits and their annual exclusions. The consent of the spouses to treat a gift as a split gift must be made on a calendar quarterly basis. The husband signifies his consent to split gifts on the wife's return, and the wife signifies her consent on the husband's return in the place provided on Form 709.

Example 2:   In January, Mr. Giving and his wife make a gift that exceeds $25,000. The decision to treat it as a split gift must be made no later than the date on which the gift tax return is filed (that is, May 15). By choosing this option, the gift to a third party is considered to be shared one-half by each spouse. Where one spouse has little or no estate, gift splitting is appropriate, since a unified estate tax credit would be wasted.

In most cases it will benefit the taxpayer to take the unified credit as soon as possible. The federal gift tax is progressive and cumulative, and there is no valid reason for saving portions of the credit for future years. By saving portions of the unified credit for future periods, gift tax rates might very well be less and therefore would reflect an illusory tax savings. But, if one considers the loss of earning power of gift taxes paid immediately as the result of any "saved" credit, then this saving will be illusionary and the net result will probably be an economic loss. The concept of the time value of money seems appropriate here in that money (or gifts) received today will be worth more than that same amount received at some future date.

A husband and wife are allowed to give away tax free an astounding amount of property in a ten-year period. If a family has four children and the spouses agree to split their gifts, a total of $591,250 can be transferred without paying any gift tax. *Each* spouse has a $47,000 (after 1980) unified credit and an annual exclusion of $3,000, which is calculated as follows.

$6,000 annual exclusion × 4 = $ 24,000 per year
                                           × 10 years
                                       $240,000
Two-exemption equivalent:
                    $175,625 × 2 = 351,250
                                       $591,250

What may be difficult to appreciate is the concept of using the unified credit as soon as possible. Other things being equal, a taxpayer should give away enough assets to use up the unified credit. Think of it as borrowing the unpaid tax from the federal government. Keep in mind that if income-producing property is given away, income can be shifted to a donee in a lower tax bracket.

A couple should not automatically elect to gift-split, especially where there is a chance that the gift will be a gift in contemplation of death. In such a situation the *full* amount of the gift (less the $3,000 exclusion) is included in the decedent's gross estate along with any gift taxes in fact paid by the decedent.

This "gross-up" does *not* include any gift tax paid by the other spouse, since the spouse's payment of such a gift tax does *not* reduce the decedent's estate at death. When the other spouse dies, one-half of the gift (less the $3,000 exclusion) is added to the second spouse's taxable estate as an "adjusted taxable gift." Although the statutes are not clear, the second spouse should receive a credit for the gift tax paid by the second spouse.

Example 3:   Husband makes a gift to his son of $200,000 and his wife agrees to gift-split. Husband includes $97,000 in taxable gifts and his wife includes $97,000 in her taxable gifts. If husband dies within three years of this gift, a total of $197,000 is includable in his gross estate under Section 2037. When wife dies, she also adds $97,000 to her adjusted taxable gift. Notice that this same gift is includable one and a half times; that is, completely in the husband's estate and one-half in the wife's estate.

Marital Deduction

Since April 2, 1948, a donor has been allowed an exemption on *separate* property which at the time of the gift belonged to the donor's spouse. In order to establish equity between separate and community-property, a donor was permitted until 1977 to deduct one-half of any gifts to his/her spouse. After 1976, there is an unlimited marital deduction for the first $100,000, and a 50 percent deduction for gifts above $200,000. Thus, a much larger amount may be given to a spouse after 1976 without paying a tax. Apparently, this $100,000 limitation is a per-donor limitation (that is, no extra amount for a second marriage).

Example 4: Husband transfers $250,000 to his spouse in 1977, his first gift to her. He would be allowed a total marital deduction of $125,000.

Community-property is not applicable to this marital deduction. In the transfer of property, the status of the donor is the critical factor (not the status of the donee). For example, a nonresident alien donor is not allowed a marital deduction, whereas a resident donor is not denied a deduction merely because the donee is a nonresident alien.

Although a "permanent interest" or present interest qualifies as a marital deduction, a "terminable interest" is not allowed. Generally speaking, a permanent interest does not cease with the death of the donee and is eventually included in the donee's gross estate unless the gift is disposed of before the donee's death. To state this another way, the donee spouse must have full power to dispose of the gift property before a marital deduction is allowed.

Two major exceptions to the terminable interest rule exist. The first exception occurs when the donee has enough control over the gift property to make the donee the owner of the property. Before this exception is applicable, these five conditions must be met:

1. The donee spouse must be entitled for life to all income from the entire interest.
2. Such income must be payable annually or at more frequent intervals.
3. The donee spouse must have the power (exercisable in favor of the donee or donee's estate) to appoint the entire interest.
4. Such a power must be exercisable by the donee spouse alone and (whether exercisable by will or during life) must be exercisable by the donee in all events.
5. No part of the entire interest must be subject to a power in any other person to appoint any part thereof to any person other than the donee spouse.

When this "life estate with power of appointment in donee spouse" occurs, the transferred property qualifies for the marital deduction.

A gift of joint interest is the other exception to the terminable interest rule. If the property is transferred to a donee spouse as a sole joint tenant with the donor or as tenant by the entirety, the interest of the donor in the gift property—which exists solely because of the possibility that the donor may survive the donee spouse, or that there may occur a severance of tenancy—can still qualify for the marital deduction. For this exception to apply, such a transfer must be between husband and wife, and the spouses must be the only joint tenants.

Under the new rules, an individual can transfer tax-free approximately $600,000 to his spouse during life and at death. This significant amount is computed as follows (assuming the individual dies after 1980):

Marital deduction (gift tax)	$175,625
Unified tax credit	175,625
Estate tax marital deduction	250,000
Total	$601,250

Of course, this sum does not include the $3,000 tax-free exclusion per year that can be given to the spouse.

Example 5: A spouse can give $357,250 to the other spouse in 1981 and thereafter without incurring a tax. This amount is composed of the unified credit of $47,000, a marital deduction of $178,625, and a $3,000 exclusion. [Solve for X in this equation: $3,000 + 175,625 + 100,000 + \frac{1}{2}(X - 200,000) = X$]

Deduction for Charitable Gifts

A deduction is allowable on the federal gift tax return for certain gifts to qualified charities (Schedule A, line (h)(1)). If the gift to the charity is $3,000 or less and is a present-interest gift, such a transfer does not have to appear on a gift tax return. However, if the gift exceeds $3,000 or is a future-interest gift, the transfer must eventually be reported on a gift tax return. However, even if the charitable gift is reported, the taxpayer is allowed a deduction for the gift (that is, a "wash" effect). A donor is required to report charitable transfers on the fourth-quarter return, or at such earlier time as he is required to file a return for a noncharitable gift. There is no percentage limitation as to the amount deductible on the gift tax return.

A "qualified charitable transfer" is defined as a transfer where a deduction is allowable under Section 2522 for the full amount of the gift. For example, if Mr. Char gives outright securities to a qualified charitable organization, he is entitled to a charitable deduction and would not have to file a special return for such gift.

But suppose Mr. Char transfers property in trust to his son for life, with the remainder to a charitable organization after his son's death. This gift would *not* be a "qualified charitable transfer," since a gift-tax charitable deduction is not allowable in an amount equal to the full amount transferred. Thus, Mr. Char must file a return reporting the entire gift to the split-interest trust by the fifteenth day of the second month following the end of the calendar quarter. Mr. Char may have to pay a gift tax for the interest transferred to his son.

Gifts made to public, religious, charitable, scientific, literary, and educational organizations (including the encouragement of arts and the prevention of cruelty to children or animals) are normally deductible. But a gift made to a public institution is deductible only if made to the United States, any state, territory, any political subdivision thereof, or the District of Columbia.

A citizen or resident is allowed a gift tax deduction for transfers to a charitable organization, regardless of whether the organization is a United

States institution or foreign institution. On the other hand, a nonresident alien may obtain a deduction only for gifts to a domestic corporation; and a nonresident alien may not deduct gifts to a foreign trust, community chest, fund, or foundation unless the gift is used within the United States for charitable purposes.

Certain deductions are disallowed for gifts to or for the use of organizations or trusts described in Section 5508(d) or Section 4948(c)(4).

A charitable deduction is allowed for certain *future* interests in property given to a charity. The future interest (except for a future interest in a personal residence or farm) must be in the form of a charitable remainder annuity trust, a charitable remainder unitrust, or a pooled income fund.[4]

Charitable remainder annuity trust is a trust that is to pay its income beneficiary (or beneficiaries) a specific sum which is not less than 5 percent of the initial fair market value of all property placed in the trust. At the death of the income beneficiary, or at the end of a term of years (not greater than 20 years), the remainder interest must be paid to a qualified organization described above.[5]

Charitable remainder unitrust is a trust that is to pay the income beneficiary (or beneficiaries) a fixed percentage which is not less than 5 percent of the net fair market value of its assets (as valued annually).[6] There are two exceptions. The trust instrument may provide (1) that the trustee is to pay the income beneficiary for any year the amount of trust income, where this amount is less than the portion required to be distributed by the particular unitrust, and (2) that the trustee is to pay the beneficiary an amount of trust income in excess of that required to be distributed, to the extent he paid less than that portion in prior years because of the requirement to pay only the amount of the trust income.[7]

Pooled income fund is similar to a charitable remainder trust except that the donor's irrevocable gifts are commingled with similar contributions in a fund maintained by the organization to which the remainder interest is contributed. This fund must meet six strict rules.[8]

So that a present interest to a charity can be deductible, it must be in the form of an annuity trust interest.

The value of the charitable deduction is computed by using the actuarial tables in Publication 723, *Valuation of Last Survivor Charitable Remainder*,[9] available from the U.S. Government Printing Office.

One other exception to this denial of a charitable deduction (where the donor retains a life interest in the property) applies to gifts of personal residences and farms. A donor may still obtain a charitable deduction for a gift to a publicly supported charity (but *not* to a trust) even though he retains a right to live in the residence or use the farm.[10] However, the law does severely restrict the contribution of future interest in personal property (for example, paintings, jewelry, antiques) where the donor wishes to retain the enjoyment of the property during his lifetime. Further, some contributions of tangible personal property to public charities result in a 50 percent reduction in the appreciation portion of the property.[11]

PRESENT vs. FUTURE INTEREST

Earlier, the criticality of determining whether a gift is a present or future interest was mentioned. This topic deserves a more thorough discussion. The definition of a present interest is an "unrestricted right to the immediate use, possession, or enjoyment of property or the income from property (such as a life estate or term certain)."

The entire amount of any gift of future interest in property must be included in "taxable gifts," with the exception of certain gifts to minors (discussed later in more detail). "Reversions, remainders, and other interests or estates, whether vested or contingent, and whether or not supported by a particular interest or estate, which are limited to commence in use, possession or enjoyment at some future date or time" are all included in the term "future interest." From a decree by the Supreme Court we find that "the critical test is whether there has been a postponement of the rights of the donees to use, possess, and enjoy the property." [12] The law has stipulated that any remainder interest, even though marketable, is a future interest.

It is advisable, then, to make sure that the gifts made are of a "present interest" if it is expected that any exclusions from the amounts of these gifts will be taken. Gifts of "present interest" are the only forms of gifts to which an exclusion can be applied. The classification of gifts as either present or future interest should be made prior to the gift by the donor so as to take the optimum advantage of the tax consequences.

Example 6:   An unmarried individual transfers assets to a trust for Sam for life, with the remainder to Deater. Sam's life estate value is $2,700 and Deater's remainder interest is worth $9,300. The taxable gift is $9,300 because there is no exclusion on the future-interest gift.

Gifts to Minors

A transfer of property by gifts to minors can be an effective planning tool. One very important exception to the future-interest rule is a transfer under the Uniform Gift to Minors Act. In a typical situation, a taxpayer irrevocably transfers securities, cash, or life insurance to a minor by registering the property in the name of the custodian designated by the donor. The donor should not be the custodian so as to insure that the given property will not be included in the donor's gross estate if he/she dies before the minor reaches the age of majority. This selection can be a very important event, since Rev. Rul. 59-357 [13] indicates that if the donor is the custodian and dies before the donee has reached the age of 21 years, it is quite likely that the gift will not be considered a future interest. This will be the case if all three of the following conditions are met:

1. Both the property and its income may be expended by or for the benefit of the donee before he attains the age of 21.
2. Any portion of the property and its income not disposed of under condition (1) will pass to the donee when he attains the age of 21 years.

3. Any portion of the property and income not disposed of under condition (1) will be payable either to the estate of the donee or to whomever he may appoint under a general power of appointment if he dies before attaining the age of 21 years.[14]

There are also other tax benefits of making a gift to minors. In 1978 a minor could receive up to $850 of dividend income tax-free (composed of the $750 personal exemption and the $100 dividend exclusion). Thus a sizable income tax savings can result from a shift of income-producing property to a child, since the minor will be in a lower tax bracket. Furthermore, such gifts can insulate assets from the grips of creditors. Where the donor has the responsibility to support the donee, this income tax savings can be diluted. Regardless of the relationship of the donor or of the custodian to the donee, income from the gift property used to discharge the donor's support obligation is taxable to the donor.

Example 7: A father transfers securities worth $90,000 to a trust for the benefit of his son Harvey. The property and income may be expended by or for the benefit of the minor prior to his attaining 21 years of age and, if not so expended, will pass to the donee upon his attaining majority, or in the event of his prior death, will be payable to his estate or to whomever he may appoint under a general power of appointment. Assuming gift splitting, the minimum taxable gift (ignoring the unified credit) is $86,000 ($90,000 − 6,000).

In a closely held corporation situation, gifts of stock may be a useful tool for family income splitting. But the donor should not retain any interest in the transferred stock and all gifts should be "for real." The Commissioner may use the general principles of the *Gregory* or *Knetsch* cases, in which the transfer of the property did not have an economic reality.[15] For example, in one court decision a father gave 25 percent of a Subchapter S corporation to each of his two minor sons. Although he filed a gift tax return, he paid no gift tax and waited one year before he typed his wife's name in as the custodian. The donor prepared and signed tax returns for the children and paid the sons' tax liabilities from his own funds. Custodian bank accounts were not established for the donees until several years later. The Tax Court ruled that the stock transfers had "no economic reality" and were thereby not bona fide.[16] As one would expect, gifts other than shares of stock must also be of economic reality.

Valuation of Gift Transfers

In order to determine "taxable gifts," a proper valuation of the gift property must be made. Gifts of money cause no valuation problems, but this is not true of gifts of property.

In general, a gift is valued at its fair market value on the date of the gift. Where property is transferred for less than adequate and full consideration, then the amount by which the fair market value of property exceeds the value of the consideration is considered to be a gift. A gift occurs even if later facts indicate that the donor never enjoyed anything possessory and did not really transfer anything. One must look to see if there was any value on the date of the gift.[17]

Regulation 25.1512-1 defines value of the property as the price at which the gift property would change hands between a willing buyer and a willing seller (that is, when neither is under the compulsion to buy or sell), and that value is not a forced sale price. Nor is the value of the gift property the sales price in a market other than that in which such an item is normally sold to the public. This means that most gifts would be valued at the price at which the item would be sold at retail. For gift tax purposes, for example, a fur coat would be valued at the price for which a coat of like description would be purchased by the general public.

Since the donor is primarily liable for the tax, the amount of the gift is the fair market value of the property passing from the donor, and is not the value of the property received by the donee. The value is generally determined at the time of the gift of each unit of property. The assessed value for state and local purposes is generally not the basis for gift tax purposes.

COMPUTING THE GIFT TAX

Although the gift tax is imposed separately in each calendar quarter on the total taxable gifts made during a given quarter, the applicable tax payable is determined by the *total of all gifts* made by the donor during that quarter and in *all* prior quarters and years. That is, the gift tax rates are cumulative and progressive. From the gift tax rate standpoint alone, there is no benefit gained by spreading gifts over a number of years; however, it may be beneficial to spread gifts over a number of years in order to take advantage of the $3,000 annual exclusion and other deductions. There are six major steps in computing the gift tax:

Step 1   Determine the amount (fair market value, FMV) of the taxable gifts for the calendar quarter for which the gift tax return is being prepared. This step is broken down into a formula below.

Step 2   Ascertain the total FMV of all taxable gifts made by the donor for all prior calendar quarters and years after June 6, 1932 (including gifts after 1976).

Step 3   Sum the amounts in steps 1 and 2. Compute the tax on this total by using the unified estate and gift tax rates.

Step 4   Compute the theoretical unified gift tax on the amount in step 2.

Step 5   Subtract the tax computed in step 4 from the tax computed in step 3 in order to determine the tentative gift tax payable.

Step 6   Subtract the applicable unified credit from the amount in step 5 to arrive at the gift tax payable.

Step 1 above can be expanded into this formula:

Gross gifts (FMV)	XX
Less: Annual exclusions, if any, of $3,000 per donee per year of present-interest gifts	X
	XX
Less other deductions:	
FMV of charitable gifts	X
Marital deduction on gifts to spouse	X
	X
Taxable gifts	XX

Notice that pre-1977 gifts are used in computing gifts for preceding quarters and calendar years. However, the *new* unified rates are used in figuring the tax on these pre-1977 gifts even though such tax is greater than the amount produced under the old rates.

Example 8: A husband made no gifts prior to 1977. In April, 1977, he makes the following gifts: $150,000 to wife, $20,000 to daughter, $30,000 to grandson, and $10,000 to a cousin. The wife does *not* gift-split with husband. The husband would be allowed a total exclusion of $12,000 and a marital deduction of $100,000, resulting in taxable gifts of $98,000 ($210,000 − 12,000 − 100,000). A tentative gift tax liability of $23,240, less the unified credit of $6,000, results in a gift tax due of $17,240.

Incomplete Gifts

A major objective of a lifetime gift is to remove the property from the gross estate of the donor. There are four major areas where this objective is not accomplished, since the gift is included in the donor's taxable estate: gifts in contemplation of death, transfers with a retained life interest, transfers taking effect at death, and revocable transfers. Each area is discussed below, with emphasis on ways of avoiding these incomplete gifts. Many transfers that are not complete for *estate* tax purposes may be complete for gift tax purposes. They are "not always mutually exclusive." [18]

GIFTS IN CONTEMPLATION OF DEATH

Under Section 2035(a), a decedent's gross estate is increased by the fair market value of all gifts that were made in contemplation of death. Prior to 1977, gifts made within three years prior to the date of the decedent's death were *presumed* to be made in contemplation of death.[19] Even if the property is sold by the donee before the donor's death, the FMV of the same property at the date of death is included. Any increase in value resulting from actions of the donee is not taken into consideration when determining the value.[20] However, if the donee has dissipated the property so that there is little left on the date of the transferor's death, the amount includable is not what actually exists, but rather is the present value of the property originally transferred.[21]

In order to overcome the three-year presumption, the administrators must show by a fair preponderance of evidence that the donor had life motives rather than death motives for making the gifts. If the donor lives three years after a gift, it is assumed that the gift was not in contemplation of death and that it is not included in his gross estate.

For gifts made after December 31, 1976, the rebuttable "gift in contemplation of death presumption" has been deleted. Instead, any gifts made by a decedent or his spouse after this date, and during the three-year period ending on the date of the decedent's death, are automatically included in the gross estate. In effect, *only the appreciation* from the date of the lifetime gift to the date of death (or six months thereafter) is included in the estate, since the original "gift" was taxed by the unified estate and gift tax system. In other words, the *date-of-gift* value is included in the estate for gifts made more than three years prior to death, whereas the *date-of-death* value of the gift is included in gross estate if it is a gift in contemplation of death.

Example 9: In 1978, Jim makes a gift to his daughter of assets worth $100,000. When Jim dies in 1981, the property is worth $170,000. Since this transfer is not a gift in contemplation of death, only $100,000 (less a $3,000 exclusion) is taxed by the unified estate tax rate. If, instead, Jim dies in 1980 (within three years after making the gift) when the assets are worth $160,000, then a total of $160,000 (less a $3,000 exclusion) is included in Jim's estate.

Example 10: Assume in Example 9 that the property is worth $60,000 when Jim dies in 1980. Only the depreciated amount of $60,000 (less a $3,000 exclusion) is included in Jim's estate. Obviously, Section 2035 is *helpful* if the property *depreciates* in value, but *harmful* if the property *appreciates* in value.

If a gift is included in the gross estate as a gift in contemplation of death, the gift must be "grossed-up." That is, the gift tax *in fact paid by the decedent or his estate* must be added back to the gift when it is included in the gross estate. However, since Section 2035 does not draw the $3,000 per donee exclusion into the gross estate, death-bed gifts up to $3,000 per donee are still valuable. For example, four death-bed gifts of $3,000 would remove $12,000 from the gross estate. In a 50 percent estate tax bracket, such gifts would result in a $6,000 tax saving. In case of gift splitting, the extra $3,000 is drawn back into the estate in the case of a gift in contemplation of death. Thus, where it appears that the donor will not live at least three years, gift splitting is not appropriate.

Even when it appears that a gift may be in contemplation of death, a gift may still be advisable. The donor may live three years; if not, he/she may be in a high-income tax bracket and the transfer can place the income-producing property in the hands of a lower-tax-bracket donee. Moreover, any gift tax paid is normally allowed as a full credit against any future estate tax, even if a spouse elects under Section 2513 to split a gift in contemplation of death.[22] In other words, the gift tax paid with respect to both halves of the gift is allowed as a credit on the donor's (decedent's) estate tax return, but there is no restoration of the unified credit used against gift taxes paid by the surviving spouse.

An unexpected gift in contemplation of death may, however, upset a marital deduction formula clause. The purpose of such a formula is to limit the amount of property passing to a surviving spouse while at the same time obtaining the maximum marital deduction. An unplanned increase in the adjusted gross estate will increase the amount that the surviving spouse receives and decrease the amount available for other heirs.

TRANSFERS WITH RETAINED LIFE INTEREST

If a donor retains a life interest in transferred property, such a transfer is not a complete transfer and will be included in the donor's estate under Section 2036(a). An interest in the property is defined as (1) the possession or enjoyment of, or the right to the income of the property; or (2) the right, whether alone or in conjunction with any person, to designate the persons who shall possess or enjoy the property or the income therefrom.[23]

The gift tax provisions do not follow the estate tax provisions. Whereas the full value of a transferred interest (where the donor has retained a life interest) is included in the gross estate upon death, such a transfer is subject to the gift tax. Of course the donor is allowed to deduct from the fair market value of the transferred property the value of the life interest retained. The difference is subject to the gift tax, and any income received by the donor is, of course, taxable income.

Example 11: Grantor transfers $320,000 of stock (adjusted basis of $140,000) to a trust, but retains power to change the beneficiaries. Although grantor may divest himself of any power to revoke the trust or to make himself a beneficiary, this is not a complete gift.

Example 12: Grantor transfers property with a reservation of a life estate. When he dies, the entire property is included in his estate. The remainder interest is valued at $123,000, and the life interest is valued at $29,000. There would be a complete gift as to the $123,000 interest.

TRANSFERS TAKING EFFECT AT DEATH

If a donor transfers property but retains a reversionary interest, such property is included in his gross estate under Section 2037(a). The gift is incomplete for estate tax purposes if three elements are present:

1. Possession or enjoyment of the property could, through ownership of the interest, have been obtained only by surviving the decedent.
2. The donor retains a reversionary interest in the transferred property. (Different rules apply for transfers before October 8, 1949.)
3. The value of the reversionary interest immediately before the donor's death exceeds 5

percent of the value of the property. The reversionary percentage is computed from the applicable actuarial tables.[24]

Such a conditional gift causes all or some of the value of the property to be included in the gross estate of the donor.

If the donor transfers the property in trust for at least ten years and one day, any income from the property escapes the income tax under Section 673(a). As for gift tax purposes, the donor must give up dominion and control over such property to escape this tax. But the estate and gift tax rules are not perfectly coordinated. As long as the donor cannot revest the interest in himself alone (or change with someone who has a substantial nonadverse interest), or dispose of the property directly for himself or others (or by an ascertainable standard by a trustee), a completed gift of all the property has occurred. Thus, if a donor retains a power exercisable only in conjunction with a person having a substantial adverse interest (even a family member), the gift is complete. Furthermore, even when a reversion is retained by the donor, such a reversion will not make the gift entirely incomplete, but it will reduce the amount of taxable gift (even if less than a 5 percent reversionary interest).[25] But where a trustee can invade corpus of a trust on behalf of the donor, the gift would be incomplete to the extent that the definite standard is enforceable.

REVOCABLE TRANSFERS

A final incomplete gift may occur when the donee's enjoyment of the transferred property is subject (at the donor's death) to any change through the exercise of a power by the donor to alter, amend, revoke, or terminate the interest. If Section 2038 is applicable, any gift property would be includable in the donor's gross estate.[26] This section does not apply if

1. Transfer was for adequate and full consideration.
2. Donor's power could be exercised only with the consent of all parties having an interest in the transferred property.
3. Power was held solely by a person other than the donor.[27]

A revocable transfer is an incomplete gift. If the power to revoke is held by the donor in conjunction with a person who has a substantial adverse interest, the gift would be incomplete. In contrast to the estate law, a reserved power to merely change the time and manner of the enjoyment of the beneficiary by the donor would not make the gift incomplete.[28] Yet a "time and manner" reserved power would draw the property into the gross estate under Section 2038. Regulation 25.2511-2(g) indicates that if a donor transfers property to himself as trustee (or to himself and some other person not possessing an adverse interest), and retains no beneficial interest in the trust property and no power over it except fiduciary powers, the exercise or nonexercise of which is limited by an ascertainable standard to change the beneficiary of such property, the donor has made a complete gift. Therefore, the gift tax consequences of a revocable gift coincide with the estate tax consequences.

Example 13: Apple transfers property worth $122,000 in trust for Karl, but reserves the power to revoke the trust with the trustee of the trust (who is unrelated to Apple or Karl). Since the trustee is not an adverse interest, this is not a complete gift.

Example 14: Barry transfers property to a trust for Yual for life, with remainder to Xexe. But Barry reserves the power to revoke the trust with the consent of Yual. If the life estate is worth $28,000 and the remainder interest is worth $93,000, only $28,000 is a complete gift.

Are Lifetime Gifts Worthwhile?

The incentive for lifetime gifts has been reduced as a result of the Tax Reform Act of 1976. There are disadvantages and advantages in making gifts after 1976.

Some disadvantages of lifetime gifts are as follows:

1. Making taxable gifts result in prepayment of the transfer tax (that is, an interest-free loan is made to the federal government).
2. Lifetime taxable gifts increase the effective unified transfer tax bracket rate at death.
3. Gifts made within three years of death are included within the gross estate with a "gross-up" for any gift taxes paid. (The $3,000 per donee exclusion is not included in the estate.)
4. To the extent that any portion of the unified credit is used against lifetime transfers, there is a reduction in the amount of the unified credit available at death. However, you may

wish to make enough gifts during life to use up your unified credit (without paying a gift tax). Thus, you will make gifts without paying a tax, which is somewhat like borrowing such a deferred gift tax payable from the federal government.

Some advantages in making lifetime gifts are as follows: Gifts

1. Eliminate future appreciation from the donor's estate.
2. Allow a donor to transfer income-producing property to beneficiaries who may be in low-income tax brackets.
3. Permit up to $3,000 per donee per year ($6,000 for married couples) and are still tax-exempt transfers.
4. Are subject to an unlimited marital deduction for the first $100,000 of lifetime gifts to a spouse, no deduction on the next $100,000, and a 50 percent deduction above $200,000.
5. Made more than three years prior to the donor's death are not "grossed-up" in the donor's estate.

As one becomes older and the value of his assets increases, a program of lifetime gifts may be beneficial. Let us assume that a wealthy married man in a high-tax bracket plans to leave a portion of his estate to his children. If the father's estate surpasses the $176,000 level, it may be advantageous for him to make gifts while he is still living. If the children who receive the gifts are in a low-tax bracket, the taxpayer may obtain both savings in income tax and also use his unified credit early by giving a portion of the assets to them. Since the children will eventually receive the assets anyway, it makes sense for the father to distribute them in the most advantageous manner. Although it may be beneficial to make gifts, findings indicate that ignorance of potential tax savings and other nontax factors are the major reasons for people not using such a valuable tax-planning tool.

REFERENCES

1. Robert W. Hite, Sr., 49 T.C. 580 (1968); see similar tests in *Lorenzo W. Swope Estate*, 41 B.T.A. 213 (1910).
2. *Robinette* v. *Helvering* 318 U.S. 184 (1943).
3. Reg. 25.2511-1(g)(1).
4. IRC Sections 170(f)(2)(a), 2055(e), 2106(a)(2)(E), and 2522(c).
5. IRC Section 664(d)(1).
6. IRC Section 664(d)(2).
7. IRC Section 664(d)(3).
8. IRC Section 642(c)(5).
9. Prop. Reg. 25.2522(c)-3(c)(2)(v).
10. IRC Sections 170(f)(3) and (4).
11. IRC Sections 170(e)(A) and (B)(ii). See chapter 9.
12. *Ryerson* v. *U.S.*, 312 U.S. 405 (1941).
13. 1959-2 C.B. 212.
14. Reg. 25.2503-4(a).
15. *Gregory* v. *Helvering*, 293 U.S. 465 (1935); *Knetsch* v. *U.S.*, 364 U.S. 361 (1960).
16. Duarte, 44 T.C. 193 (1965). See Crumbley and Davis, *Organizing, Operating, and Terminating Subchapter S Corporations* (Tucson, Ariz.: Lawyers & Judges Publishing Co., 1977).
17. *Goodwin* v. *McGowan*, 47 F. Supp. 798 (W.D. N.Y. 1942).
18. *Estate of Stanford* v. *U.S.*, 308 U.S. 45 (1939).

19. Section 2035(b).

20. Reg. 20.2035-1(e).

21. *Humphrey Estate* v. *Commissioner*, 162 F.2d 1 (1947), cert. den 332 U.S. 817.

22. Reg. 20.2012-1(e).

23. Sections 2036(a)(1) and (2).

24. Prop. Reg. 25.2512-5(f).

25. Reg. 25.2511-1(e).

26. Section 2038(a); *Burnet* v. *Guggenheim,* 288 U.S. 280 (1933).

27. Reg. 20.2038-1(a).

28. Reg. 25.2511-2(d).

7

Trusts and Estates

The time will come when the poor man
will not be able to wash his shirt
without paying a tax.
A Congressman in 1790

ONE of the basic purposes of estate planning is to pass the benefits of accumulated wealth from one family member to another in a manner conducive to the best interests of the estate owner and with a minimum reduction of that wealth from taxes. Some of the most important advantages of trusts are derived from the fact that trusts are based upon the concepts of property arrangement and property management. Therefore, trust departments are primarily interested in selling the trust device as a means of preserving property and as a means of efficiently administering the family assets for the benefit of the beneficiaries.

The trust instrument is a valuable tool in estate planning, primarily because it permits considerable flexibility in the disposition and administration of property. The trust device not only saves taxes, but also provides the flexibility needed to achieve many of the nontax objectives. Often such things as prudent management of assets and the ability to give someone (the trustee) the right to use discretion as to the amount and timing of income and principal distributions are just as important as the savings of taxes.

Since the trust provides so many opportunities and advantages in estate planning, no estate plan should be adopted until full consideration is given to the possibility of using a trust (or trusts) to carry out one or more of the desires of the estate owner. This chapter presents a brief introduction to trusts in general, to different classifications of trusts, and to some of the uses of trusts in estate planning.

INTRODUCTION TO TRUSTS

Before there can be any meaningful discussion of a trust, one must be familiar with the term, its definition, and its characteristics. One should also be familiar with the basic purposes for which trusts may be and are established. This section of the chapter contains a discussion of the definition, characteristics, and purposes of a trust.

Definitions and Characteristics of Trusts

The term "trust" is used by courts and lawyers in a variety of senses. Often it is used to include other fiduciary relationships such as bailments, executorships, guardianships, and agencies. However, in a narrower sense, the term is applied to a particular kind of fiduciary relationship that began in England when the courts of law and courts of equity in that country were separated. In this book, the term "trust" is applied only to trusts in this narrower sense.

Because of the way in which our laws are structured, a definition of any legal concept cannot properly be used as though it were a major premise so that rules governing conduct can be deduced from it. Since there is not one exact or perfect definition of the term "trust," several definitions are given in an attempt to acquaint the reader with the legal concept. One author defines a trust as a fiduciary relationship in which one person holds property, subject to an equitable obligation to keep or use such property for the benefit of another person.[1] In its *Restatement of the Law*, the American Law Institute defined a trust as a fiduciary relationship with respect to property, subjecting the person holding title to the property to equitable duties in dealing with the property for the benefit of another person. This relationship arises as a result of a manifestation of an intention to create it.[2] Another writer defines a trust as a relationship between a trustee and a beneficiary with respect to rights in property, where legal ownership is divorced from equitable ownership and legal title is held by the trustee exclusively for the benefit of the beneficiary because of the latter's equitable interest.[3] At least one court has defined a trust as a property right held by one party for the use of another.[4]

These definitions of the term *trust* (and many others) seem concerned with the duty or obligation of the trustee, or with the rights of the beneficiary, rather than the nature of a trust. The trust in its modern sense is conceived to be the relationship in which the trustee holds the trust property subject to the trust agreement for the benefit of the beneficiaries.

Even though the preceding definitions are not exact or perfect, certain characteristics of a trust may be derived from them. These characteristics are (1) a trust is a relationship; (2) it is a relationship of a fiduciary character; (3) it is a relationship with respect to property; (4) it involves the existence of equitable duties imposed upon the trustee for the benefit of the beneficiaries; and (5) it arises as a result of a clear intention to create the relationship. These characteristics give rise to our modern day meaning of the term *trust*.

A trust is a relationship with respect to property held by the trustee. Such property is referred to as "the trust property." The trust property may be defined as the interest in a thing—real or personal, tangible or intangible—which the trustee holds, subject to the rights of another.[5] Besides the trust property, the relationship usually involves three parties. The settlor (or grantor) of the trust is the person who creates or intentionally causes it to come into existence. Some other terms used to designate the settlor are *trustor, grantor,* and *donor.* The beneficiary is the person entitled to the benefits from the trust property. The third party to the trust is the trustee, who holds the legal title to the trust property for the benefit of the beneficiary.

In a fiduciary relationship, the law demands that one party of such a relationship must have an unusually high standard of ethical or moral conduct with respect to another party of the relationship. In a trust, the trustee is the one required to have such characteristics. It is his duty to represent and act solely in the interest of the beneficiary; he is not permitted to consider his own personal needs or desires. Due to the nature of a trust and the trustee's control over the trust property, he/she is expected to apply more than casual consideration and judgment in dealings with the beneficiary.

The settlor, in creating a trust, can state the necessary provisions with respect to the duties and powers of the trustee and the rights of the beneficiaries; unless these provisions are contrary to any local policy or law, they are valid and enforceable. Most of the legal principles and rules governing trusts are applicable only if the settlor does not provide otherwise. Thus, an estate planner must be familiar with trust law and know exactly what a particular trust can and cannot do before attempting to use it in an estate plan.

Purposes of Trusts

Trusts originated in England in the fifteenth century as an attempt to alleviate some of the rigid burdens of the common law. These trusts usually required the person who had legal right to the property to exercise the benefits of the property to whomever was equitably entitled to it. The usefulness of the trust concept became so apparent that it has been extended over the centuries and is still quite popular and useful today.

The trust concept has been utilized in many kinds of arrangements, such as a substitute for incorporation (the Massachusetts trust), real estate holdings, voting trusts, support of charities, and reserves set up for creditors. But the widest and most important use of trusts is in the field of family settlements. As the character of property ownership has changed, trusts have been established more and more to manage property other than land. As a result, most personal trusts at the present time consist of securities of one kind or another. But the basic purpose remains the same—the protection of the financial interests of the family.

INTRODUCTION TO ESTATES

Rather than eliminating taxation, death of an individual incurs several new tax responsibilities. For example, assume an individual dies on July 12. The executor must file tax returns for two separate entities. A regular Form 1040 return must be filed for the period before his death, including the date of his death (that is, July 12). Further, Form 1041 (estate income tax) must include any income or deductions that occur after the death. Of course, if the estate is large enough, a federal estate tax is due on Form 706.

If the gross income of the estate is $600 or more, or any beneficiary is a nonresident alien, the fiduciary must file Form 1041. The fiduciary may adopt a calendar year or a fiscal year. The calculation of estate income is similar to the calculation of trust income. The tax rates used for both estate and trust income are the rates that apply to married individuals filing separate returns. The remainder of this chapter discusses the tax aspects of an estate or trust.

TAXATION OF ESTATES AND TRUSTS

Any discussion of estate and trust taxation should begin with Sections 102(a) and 102(b). Section 102(a) provides the general rule that "gross income does *not* include the value of property acquired by gift, bequest, devise, or inheritance." Section 102(b) indicates that subsection (a) "does not exclude from gross income

1. The *income* from any property referred to in subsection (a), or
2. Where the gift, bequest, devise, or inheritance is of *income* from property, the amount of such income."

Generally, most people take for granted that any distributions from an estate or trust should be considered "income from property." But this same section indicates that "any amount included in the gross income of a beneficiary under Subchapter J shall be treated for purpose of paragraph (2) as a gift, bequest, devise, or inheritance of *income* from property." The key word is, of course, "income." What the Code giveth it taketh away!

Subchapter J fills in this gap between Code Sections 102(a) and (b). In essence, the distribution rules of Sections 661 and 662 to a great extent neutralize the favorable treatment outlined in Section 102(a). The net result is that most distributions from an estate or trust are treated as taxable income, since they are considered an inheritance (or gift) of *income* under Section 102(b). There are two major safety valves:

1. Distributions that exceed distributable net income (DNI) are considered to be a tax-free transfer of income under Section 102(a).
2. A specific bequest of an amount of money or property under Section 663(a)(1) is not caught by the distribution rules in Subchapter J (that is, not taxable).

Mechanical Tax Rules

The taxation aspect of an estate or trust involves a number of unique concepts:

1. Fiduciary accounting income (FAI), Section 643(b).
2. Federal gross and net income of the trust, Section 61.
3. Tentative taxable income, Sections 643(a), 61, and 63.
4. Distributable net income (DNI), Section 643(a).
5. Distribution deduction (DD) or Section 651 deduction, Section 651(a) and (b).
6. Taxable income of the trust, Sections 641(b), 642, 61, and 63.
7. Adjusted gross income to the beneficiary, Section 652(a).

The term "fiduciary accounting income" (FAI) is not defined in the statutes. Instead, Section 643(b) indicates that FAI is to be determined on a state-by-state basis, since it is "determined under the terms of the governing instrument and applicable state statutes." Anounts realized from the sale or disposition of the corpus property are allocated generally to the trust (or principal), and day-by-day income items flowing into the trust (or estate) are allocated to fiduciary accounting income (that is, taxable interest, dividends, rent income, tax-exempt interest, and so on). Keep in mind that the trust instrument or will may alter the allocation of these income items. The amount designated as FAI is, of course, the amount required to be distributed to beneficiaries, in the care of a simple trust.

Federal interpretation of the gross income of an estate or trust is determined under Section 61, the same income-determination statute for other entities. Next, a figure called "tentative taxable income" is calculated under Sections 61, 63, and 643(a). As indicated in the prologue to Section 643(a), tentative taxable income is the starting point for calculating distributable net income.

Example 1:   Assume the following facts with respect to a calendar-year simple trust with two equal beneficiaries. No provision is made for a depreciation deduction. If the long-term capital gain (LTCG) is allocated to corpus, the appropriate calculations are provided below.

Calculations for Example 1

Taxable dividends	$4,000
Rental income	4,000
Taxable bond interest	1,000
Tax-exempt interest	1,000
Long-term capital gain	2,000
Trustee commissions	$ 400 (to corpus)
Trustee commissions	500 (to income)
Rental expenses	1,500 (to income)
Tax-exempt expenditures	100 (to corpus)
Depreciation	1,000 (no provision)

Fiduciary Accounting Income

Dividends		$ 4,000
Rental income		4,000
Taxable interest		1,000
Tax-exempt interest		1,000
		$10,000
Less:		
Trustee commissions	$ 500	
Rental expenses	1,500	2,000
FAI		$ 8,000

Gross Income

Dividends		$ 3,900 *
Rental income		4,000
Taxable interest		1,000
LCTG		2,000
		$10,900

Tentative Taxable Income

Gross income		$10,900
Less:		
Capital gain deduction	$1,000	
Rental expenses	1,500	
Personal exemption	300	
Trustee commissions	810 †	3,610
TTI		$ 7,290

* After the $100 dividend exclusion.

† The trustee commissions related to tax-exempt income are not deductible. The formula is: (tax-exempt income/gross FAI) × trustee commission = amount not deductible. Therefore: (1,000/10,000) × 900 = $90; 900 − 90 = $810.

Under Section 643(a), tentative taxable income is modified in order to arrive at distributable net income (DNI). These modifications include the following:

1. No reduction of DNI for the distribution deduction.

2. No personal exemption is allowable.
3. Gains from the sale or exchange of capital assets are excluded to the extent that such gains are allocable to corpus.
4. Extraordinary dividends and taxable stock dividends are excluded when dealing with a simple trust.
5. Tax-exempt interest is included in DNI, but is reduced by any deductions associated with the tax-exempt interest. Notice that the law mentions tax-exempt interest, but not other tax-free income. For example, a tax-free stock dividend is not included in DNI.[6]
6. Special rules apply to a foreign trust.
7. The $100 dividend exclusion is included in DNI.

This artificial concept of DNI is somewhat peculiar to fiduciary taxation. DNI acts as a limitation to the amount of income that can be taxed to a beneficiary when a distribution is made. The DNI amount also provides a limitation on the distribution deduction (DD) in order to stop tax avoidance through unlimited accumulation of income and use of gifts to charitable remainders. Think of DNI as a *quantitative* concept for measuring the amount of income taxable to an estate or trust.

The distribution deduction (DD) is in most situations a modified DNI. In order to avoid double taxation to an estate or trust, the statutes provide a deduction for purposes of computing the taxable income of the fiduciary, where income is distributed currently to the beneficiaries. This DD is the smaller of (1) the FAI required to be distributed currently (Section 651(a)); or (2) modified DNI (Section 651(b)). This "modified DNI" is DNI *less* any nontaxable income included in the DNI.

Example 2: Using the same facts as in Example 1, DNI may be calculated as follows, starting with tentative taxable income:

Tentative taxable income		$7,290
Personal exemption	$ 300	
Remainder of capital gain	(1,000)	
Tax-exempt interest	810 *	
Dividend exclusion	100	+ 210
		$7,500

* $1,000 less $90 applicable to trustee commissions *less* the $100 tax-exempt expenditures.

Consider DD as a *qualitative* concept for determining the characterization of income items included in the beneficiary's adjusted gross income.

Example 3: As in previous examples, DD is the smaller of (1) FAI required to be distributed, $8,000; or (2) modified DNI, $7,500 − $910 ($810 + $100) = $6,590. Thus, the amount $6,590 is used as a deduction on the trust (or estate) tax return, and is the largest amount that can be taxable to the beneficiaries.

Section 641(b) indicates that "taxable income of an estate or trust shall be computed in the same manner as in the case of an individual, except as otherwise provided in this part." Section 642 follows with special rules for credits and deductions involving an estate or trust. Thus, both Sections 61 (income) and 63 (deductions) are applicable to fiduciary taxation. Some major exceptions between an individual taxpayer and a fiduciary entity are:

1. A standard deduction is unavailable.
2. Expenditures are not divided into deductions for adjusted gross income and deductions from adjusted gross income.
3. There is no percentage-of-income limitation on charitable contributions.
4. A simple trust is allowed a $300 personal exemption; a complex trust is allowed a $100 personal exemption. A $600 personal exemption is available to an estate.
5. A trust or estate is allowed the special distribution deduction (DD) to the extent that distributions are made to the beneficiaries in order to avoid double taxation.

Example 4:   Using the facts given in the previous examples, taxable income of the trust may be calculated as follows, starting with the gross income figure from Example 1:

Gross income		$10,900
Less:		
Rental expenses	$1,500	
Capital gain exclusion	1,000	
Distribution deduction	6,590	
Trustee commissions	810	
Personal exemption	300	10,200
		$ 700

Keep in mind that this $700 amount is basically one-half of the long-term capital gain ($1,000), less the $300 personal exemption.

Section 652(a) indicates that the FAI required to be distributed currently by a simple trust * is to be

---

* A simple trust is defined as a trust in which all income is required to be distributed currently, does not distribute more than its current income, and has no charitable beneficiaries. All other trusts are complex trusts.

"included in the gross income of the beneficiaries to whom the income is required to be distributed, whether distributed or not." If FAI exceeds DNI, the amount included in the gross income of each beneficiary is the figure that bears the same ratio to DNI as the amount of FAI required to be distributed to such beneficiary bears to the total amount of FAI required to be distributed to all beneficiaries. In arithmetic terms, this figure is:

$$\frac{\text{Amount of FAI to beneficiary}}{\text{Total FAI}} \times \text{DNI}$$

Section 652(b) indicates that the character of the income in the hands of the beneficiaries is the same as in the hands of the trust.

Example 5: Assuming there are two equal beneficiaries in the previous distribution, the amount of $2,745 would be included in the adjusted gross income (AGI) of both beneficiaries. Notice in the table below that the entire rental expense (a direct expense) is allocated to the rental income.

	Rent Income	Divi- dends	Interest	Tax- exempt Interest	Total
Gross income	$4,000	$4,000	$1,000	$1,000	$10,000
Rental expense	1,500	—	—	—	1,500
Trustee commissions	810	—	—	90	900
Tax-exempt expenses	—	—	—	100	100
Total expenses	2,310	—	—	190	2,500
Total distribution	$1,690	$4,000	$1,000	$ 810	$ 7,500
	0.50	0.50	0.50	0.50	0.50
Prorata distribution	$ 845	$2,000	$ 500	$ 405	$ 3,750

Of the total $3,750 of potential gross income to a one-half beneficiary, $405 is nontaxable income.

Thus, adjusted gross income of the beneficiary is calculated as follows:

Potential DNI	$3,750
Nontaxable	−405
	$3,345
Dividend exclusion	−100
	$3,245
Depreciation expense	−500
Into AGI	$2,745

DEPRECIATION EXPENSE PROVISION

Whether or not an executor provides for a depreciation expense provision affects the calculation of the items listed above. If a depreciation reserve is not set up by the executor, FAI will be higher (to the extent of no depreciation deduction), which in turn affects the amount to be distributed. Since FAI must be distributed in a simple trust situation, the fact that no reserve is established reduces the principal (that is, the corpus of trust). In essence, the current beneficiaries receive a distributed part of the corpus. Where a trust is involved with a principal beneficiary and a remainder beneficiary, the "corpus" is being distributed to the primary beneficiary, and eventually there may be no corpus left for the secondary beneficiary. Obviously, a remainder beneficiary would prefer that a depreciation reserve be established in order to protect the corpus.

If the executor does not establish a depreciation reserve, the depreciation deduction "flows outside" FAI, DNI, and DD, and is taken as a deduction by the beneficiaries. In Example 5, no reserve was established. Thus, the $500 depreciation expense deduction did *not* decrease FAI, DNI, and DD.

Therefore, $500 more was distributed to the beneficiary. Of course, eventually, the beneficiary was able to deduct the $500 depreciation expense.

If a depreciation reserve had been established by the executor, then FAI, DNI, and DD would have been $500 less than shown in Example 5. More importantly, there would be $500 less of FAI to be distributed to the beneficiary. Thus, the reserve protects corpus from being distributed to the beneficiaries.

COMPLEX TRUSTS

The previous discussion has been limited to the taxation aspects of a simple trust. Although there are different sections in the statutes covering complex trusts, the basic rules applicable to a complex trust are the same as those for simple trusts and estates.

REFERENCES

1. George C. Bogert and George T. Bogert, *The Law of Trusts and Trustees*, 2nd ed. (St. Paul, Minn.: West Publishing Co., 1965), sec. 1.
2. American Law Institute, *Restatement of the Law, Second, Trusts*, 2d ed., Vol. I (St. Paul, Minn.: American Law Institute Publishers, 1959), Section 2.
3. Ralph A. Newman, *Newman on Trusts*, 2d ed. (Brooklyn, N.Y.: The Foundation Press, Inc., 1953), pp. 3–4.
4. *Keplinger* v. *Keplinger*, 1916, 113 N.E. 292, 293, 185 Ind. 81.
5. Bogert and Bogert, *op. cit.*, sec. 1.
6. See Section 305(a) and Rev. Rul. 67-117, 1967-1 C.B. 161.

8

Using Trusts
in Estate Planning

*In levying taxes and in shearing sheep,
it is well to stop when you get down to the skin.*
Austin O'Malley

TRUSTS may be classified in many different ways:
as to purpose, as to manner of creation, or as to revocable versus irrevocable. There are also other
ways to classify trusts. Several classifications, in addition to those just mentioned, are discussed below.

CLASSIFICATIONS OF TRUSTS

Classified as to Purpose

There are many purposes for which trusts are
formed. In fact, a trust may be created to achieve

142

any desired objective as long as the objective is not illegal or contrary to any public policy or rule of law. Some of the more common types of trusts classified as to purpose include insurance trusts, support trusts, charitable trusts, and marital deduction trusts.

CHARITABLE TRUSTS

Trusts that are originated in an effort to make one or more gifts to a charitable organization are charitable trusts. The purpose of a charitable trust is to bring social benefits to some portion of the public.[1] The American Law Institute defines charitable purposes as "(a) the relief of poverty; (b) the advancement of education; (c) the advancement of religion; (d) the promotion of health; (e) governmental or municipal purposes; and (f) other purposes, the accomplishment of which is beneficial to the community." [2]

A more thorough definition of a charitable trust appears in the *Restatement of the Law, Trusts* by the American Law Institute:

> A charitable trust is a trust the performance of which will, in the opinion of the court of chancery, accomplish a substantial amount of social benefit to the public or some reasonably large class thereof.

> It is immaterial that the settlor had personal motives in creating the trust, if the trust has charitable effects, but the purpose must not include profit-making by the settlor, trustees, or others.

> A charitable trust is to be distinguished from an absolute gift to a charitable corporation.

> A trust for "benevolent" objects may be declared a valid charitable trust, if the word "benevolent" is used as a synonym of "charitable" but not if "benevolent" is

construed as meaning any object which indicates merely goodwill toward mankind or merely liberality.[3]

The fundamental distinction between private trusts and charitable trusts is that private trusts have as their objectives the furnishing of financial benefits to individuals or corporations, whereas the charitable trust is used to benefit the general public or some large portion of the general public.

In practice, charitable trusts generally are of two types. In the first type, the charity is to receive the remainder interest of the trust after some noncharitable beneficiary has received the income from the trust for some period of time. In the second type of arrangement, the charity receives the income for a period of years, with the remainder returning to the grantor or some other designated beneficiary.

Also, consideration should be given to the tax effects of charitable trusts. If the settlor established the trust during his lifetime, he receives an income tax deduction. (See Chapter 9.) On the other hand, if the trust is established by a will or as a testamentary transfer, the settlor could receive an estate tax deduction. Thus, careful consideration must be given to the types of transfers that should be made, if the estate planner's client wants to make a gift to a charitable organization.

INSURANCE TRUSTS

The use of the trust for the disposition of life insurance proceeds is a comparatively new development. However, life insurance trusts today have become a significant part of estate planning. A personal life insurance trust is primarily an arrangement whereby the proceeds of life insurance are to be held, invested, and managed by a trustee for the benefit of the beneficiary. Such a trust may be created by the estate owner's will (testamentary) or by a lifetime gift (*inter vivos*).

Often assets other than the proceeds of life insurance are used as part of the corpus of such trusts. In fact, a trust of other property may constitute the vehicle for receiving and administering life insurance proceeds that mature upon the death of the insured. Thus, in a great many instances, a trust of life insurance proceeds is merged with a trust of other property. Such an arrangement constitutes the so-called *pour-over* method of implementing an estate plan.

Under the pour-over method, the will instructs the executor to collect all of the probate assets and pay all debts, expenses, and taxes. Next, the executor pours over all remaining assets into a trust—possibly an insurance trust. The trust, under the direction of a trustee, takes over the function of disposing of the assets in the estate.

SUPPORT TRUSTS

In our society, it is generally deemed proper to want to help our family. Many times, however, it is not desirable to pass legal title to these beneficiaries. This procedure is especially true if the beneficiaries are minors, aged, surviving spouses, or incompetents who may not be capable of properly managing the property. If the taxpayer's objective is merely to support the beneficiary, a trust may offer certain advantages over an outright transfer of property or funds used to support the beneficiary. One of the main income tax advantages of using a trust is that all the income may pass through the trust to the beneficiary and the corpus returns to the grantor at the expiration of the trust.

A trust that is designed to provide support for the beneficiary is a *support trust*. This arrangement is designed to support a beneficiary who may be incapable of handling his own financial affairs. In other words, the trust funds are protected against the beneficiary's incapacity as well as against claims from creditors.

Another type of support trust is the *short-term* or *Clifford trust* (that is, one created for at least ten years). This type is especially advantageous when the grantor is in a high-income tax bracket, but wants the corpus to return to him at the end of ten years or more. The Clifford trust offers many tax advantages and should be given careful consideration by the estate planner, especially in situations that call for support trusts.

GRANDFATHER AND EDUCATIONAL TRUSTS

Still another type of trust is the *grandfather trust*. Here the grantor creates a trust providing for income to a son (daughter) for life, with the remainder to a grandson (granddaughter). An *educational trust* is a form of support trust. A parent in a high-income tax bracket is able to transfer income-producing assets to a trust for the educational benefit of children. As long as the income is not used for the "support of the children," the income is taxed at a much lower rate in the trust or in the hands of the children.

Another form of educational trust occurs when an employer makes contributions to a trust on behalf of an employee's children. These contributions and the accumulated income are used for the children's college education. A significant deferral of income taxes occurs, since the contributions are not taxed to the employee until payments are made toward the education of the children. Of course the corporation is not allowed a deduction until a corresponding amount is included in the gross income of the participating employee.[4]

MARITAL DEDUCTION TRUSTS

The two most widely used methods of securing the marital deduction are an outright bequest to the surviving spouse or the creation of a trust from which he/she is entitled to the lifetime income and has enough control over the corpus to make it includable in his/her gross estate at death. Taking advantage of the marital deduction has two primary advantages: (1) the surviving spouse is relieved of management duties, which are shifted to the trustee, who would normally be much more proficient at managing the trust property than the surviving spouse. (2) Perhaps the most important advantage is that the trust may be set up in such a way that the surviving spouse would have to take positive action to prevent the remainder of the trust from passing to beneficiaries designated by the deceased spouse and creator of the trust.

For instance, the trust could be established so that the surviving spouse is to receive the income for life and have a general power of appointment with respect to the corpus, but if such power is not exercised, the remainder passes to the beneficiaries specified by the settlor. Because of the advantages discussed above and the fact that the marital deduction allows the estate owner to pass at least half of this adjusted gross estate to the surviving spouse tax-free, it should be obvious that the marital deduction trust should be given careful consideration by the estate planner.

Frequently two trusts are established: a marital deduction trust and a nonmarital trust. The will instructs the executor to pay $250,000 or one-half of the adjusted gross estate, whichever is greater, to the surviving spouse either directly or in a trust (called Part A). The remaining assets pass to a nonmarital trust (Part B) to be held for the benefit of the surviving spouse. Various "sprinkling provisions" can be established to allow the trustee to invade corpus for the surviving spouse or for the remainder person (often children). Of course, when the surviving spouse dies, the assets in the nonmarital trust pass tax-free to the children.

Classified as to Manner of Creation

Trusts are classified according to the manner of their creation as either made during the settlor's lifetime (*inter vivos*) or upon his/her death by a will (testamentary). An *inter vivos* or living trust is administered by the trustee, not only during the lifetime of the settlor but usually also after his death. On the other hand, a testamentary trust takes effect only upon his death.

LIVING TRUSTS

An *inter vivos* trust may either be revocable or irrevocable. The revocable *inter vivos* trust is one wherein the settlor reserves the power to terminate the trust at any time during his or her lifetime or to otherwise change its terms. Therefore, the settlor has the ability to completely cancel the trust or is at liberty to change the disposition of either the principal or income, or both, as circumstances change during his or her lifetime.

An irrevocable trust is just what the word "irrevocable" means. Once it is created, the trust agreement cannot be revoked and usually cannot be changed or modified. This means that no beneficiaries may be eliminated and no new beneficiaries may be added.

There are a number of advantages of a living trust during the settlor's lifetime:

1. It is an easy way to have one's investments managed by a financial expert, to the extent desired.

2. It is a simple, expeditious, and inexpensive way of providing for the payment of bills for one's care if one becomes sick or incapacitated, thereby avoiding the need for a conservator or guardian of the estate.

3. It gives a settlor and his family the opportunity to get acquainted with the trustee and to observe how he/she operates, and, if dissatisfied, to replace.

4. It serves as a good means of describing and segregating property according to its nature, the title thereto, and the disposition to be made of it in accordance with sound estate-planning practices.[5]

Some of the advantages of a living trust after the settlor's death include:

1. The trust assets do not become part of the decedent's probate estate and are not included in figuring the executor's commission or his attorney's fees.

2. Succeeding beneficiaries can receive trust income and principal immediately after the settlor's death unless tax consideration or the need to obtain releases cause delays.

3. A living trust has elements of privacy and confidentiality not afforded by a will because the public does not have access to the trust document or trust assets, as they do to the probate and court records.

4. The settlor, no matter where he/she lives, as well as the trustee can ordinarily choose the state law that governs the trust, whereas a will must be probated in the state and county of domicile.[6]

TESTAMENTARY TRUST

The testamentary trust is usually created by the will of the settlor and therefore does not take effect until death. One of the advantages of this type of trust is that the settlor has complete control and authority over the trust property until death. Also, testamentary trusts are established for a variety of other reasons: doubt as to the ability of beneficiaries to manage the property; a desire to keep the property away from the present or future spouses of the settlor's children; or the need for keeping a business interest under continuous management. But probably the most compelling reasons for establishing testamentary trust, at least in recent years, are based on tax plans. The most common of the tax plans is to have the property pass free of tax on the death of the surviving spouse.

Revocable versus Irrevocable Trusts

People today are unduly tax conscious. Too often the only factor that they consider is whether or not there will be a tax savings and, if so, how much it will be. However, in estate planning of revocable and irrevocable trusts, the nontax considerations can be more important than the tax considerations. This characteristic (revocable vs. irrevocable) is very important to the estate planner.

CHARACTERISTICS OF THE TWO TYPES

Generally, the irrevocable *inter vivos* trust is a vehicle for federal tax savings, while the revocable *inter vivos* trust is more suited for nontax objectives. The choice depends on the settlor's decision— either to transfer the property away forever (irrevocable) or to retain the right to get it back at a later date if he should change his mind (revocable).

The value of the revocable trust is appreciated only when one realizes that it is not permanently binding like an irrevocable *inter vivos* trust, but is, in effect, a will. For the purposes of this chapter, "revocable *inter vivos* trust" is defined as a trust created during the settlor's lifetime in which "the settlor alone has the power to revoke and in which effect of his revocation is to force the return of the corpus to himself or to force the payment of the corpus as he may direct." [7]

The basic distinction between a revocable trust and a will, both created during the settlor's lifetime, is that the former effects a present transfer of property rights subject to "divestment" by exercise of the power of revocation. The will, until the taxpayer's death, creates only an expectancy. The fundamental advantage of a will seems to be that it enables the testator to determine who shall succeed to his property after his death without requiring to part with it during his life.

The main disadvantage is that the testator's freedom of disposition is often restricted. However, it is well settled that one has much greater freedom of alienation *inter vivos* than he has freedom of testamentary disposition.[8] Because the revocable *inter vivos* trust effects a present transfer of property rights, it should not be subject to the restrictions on testamentary dispositions. However, because the trust is revocable, the settlor does not run the risk of being unable to recall the property once transferred. There are also advantages to be considered after the death of the settlor.

PROBATE RESTRICTIONS

A revocable *inter vivos* trust that continues after the settlor's death provides for an uninterrupted management arrangement. During the time of existence of the trust prior to death, the settlor has the opportunity to observe the management ability of the trustee and thus be assured that his directions will be followed.

Probate assets of a decedent are more or less in a suspended state until the executor can satisfy the claims of creditors and death-tax obligations. The potential personal liability of the executor naturally defers the availability of the use of the estate assets by the beneficiaries until such liability is eliminated.

Also, probate property and its destination are revealed in a decedent's will, and the amount and nature are generally a matter of public record. The decedent may desire to keep his financial records and method of caring for his family from becoming a part of such record, and to a considerable degree this may be accomplished by an arrangement that avoids probate, which is usually a trust property arrangement. However, the items in the gross estate (probate and nonprobate) will be disclosed in the federal estate-tax return. Also, the instrument creating a revocable *inter vivos* trust will be filed with the return. However, the return and accompanying papers are not open to public scrutiny as are probate records.[9]

Various state laws may impose upon the freedom of a property holder to decide who will be beneficiaries of his/her estate. To the extent that these restrictions apply only to probate property, they can be minimized by avoiding probate. To the extent that they are not limited to probate property, they may be avoided by placing the property under the jurisdiction of a more favorable state. Such a state may be selected by a property holder to establish a revocable *inter vivos* trust with the intention that its law control the trust, provided the trustee and the property are located there.

TAX ADVANTAGES AND DISADVANTAGES

Although the main advantages of the revocable trust are nontax considerations, a brief look at the tax situation is helpful. The Internal Revenue Code deals with taxation of trust income over which the settlor has a power of revocation. Section 676(a) provides as follows:

> The grantor shall be treated as the owner of any portion of a trust, whether or not he is treated as such owner under any other provision of the part, where at any time the power to revest in the grantor title to such portion is exercisable by the grantor or a non-adverse party or both.

Thus, under this section, income from the revocable trust property is taxed to the settlor just as if he had never made the transfer to the trustee. There is a possible method of avoiding this income tax. Section 676(b) provides:

> The income of a revocable trust shall not be taxed to the settlor if he cannot exercise the power of revocation affecting the beneficial enjoyment of the income until the expiration of a period of ten years from the date of the transfer in trust. But the settlor may be treated as the owner of the income after such a period unless the power is relinquished.

Therefore, if the settlor suspends his power of revocation for a period of more than ten years from the date on which the trust was created (that is, a Clifford trust), the trust income for such a period will not be taxed to him. However, the income will become taxable to the settlor beginning with the date on which the power of revocation becomes exercisable unless he relinquishes the power. This treatment is quite in contrast to the irrevocable trust examined below. *Warning:* Income from a trust may be taxable to the settlor to the extent such income is used to discharge a legal obligation of the settlor (that is, care of minor children).[10]

There is a major exception to the ten-year rule. The term of a Clifford trust can be limited to the life of the beneficiary even when the life expectancy of the beneficiary is less than ten years.[11]

DISADVANTAGES OF IRREVOCABLE *Inter Vivos* TRUSTS

It has already been pointed out that the principal advantage of an irrevocable *inter vivos* trust is the saving of federal income and estate taxes. The major disadvantage of such a trust stems from the fact that it results in the settlor's losing control of the property. Once made, the settlor of an irrevocable *inter vivos* trust can no longer change the terms of the trust to take into account any changed circumstances.

There may be instances when an individual would transfer property to an irrevocable *inter vivos* trust where the tax considerations are secondary. Suppose a person has accumulated an estate adequate enough to provide what he desires for his family, and realizes that he is reaching an age at which he might not be able to trust himself to make good business decisions. If he makes the trust revocable, he might unwisely revoke the trust, but if it is irrevocable, he has protected himself against this possibility.[12]

Usually, however, when a settlor decides to create an *inter vivos* trust other than a revocable one, he desires to accomplish the two following tax results:

1. The income from the trust will be removed from his taxable income; and

2. The appreciation value that occurs after the transfer of the trust property will be removed from his gross estate.

The cost of accomplishing these results is mainly that the unified tax credit must be used, or, if the trust property is sufficiently large, the payment of a federal transfer tax must be made early. Considering other economic factors related to a reduction in one's wealth, a gift can still be a sound device for estate planning.

The property owner, by making outright gifts during his lifetime, shifts the income tax liability from himself to the person to whom he makes the gift. Thus, if he makes an irrevocable gift in trust, he may, according to the terms of the trust, shift the income tax liability to the trust or to the beneficiary. If the income is not distributed or is not distributable, it is taxable to the trust. If it is distributed or distributable, ordinarily it is taxable to the beneficiary. But, although the trust is irrevocable, the property owner may have reserved the right to leave himself substantially the owner of the property, in which case the income would be taxable to him.

A trust under which the settlor retains the right to the income for life, with the remainder to someone else but which cannot be revoked, creates a situation that reduces the gross estate only by the amount of the gift tax paid (if any). The settlor is taxable on the income from such a trust because he has the right to receive it, and the value of the principal of such a trust is includable in his gross estate for federal estate tax purposes. Thus, there is no major tax advantage to be gained by using such a trust.[13]

Sections 671–677 of the Internal Revenue Code spell out in detail the circumstances under which the settlor would be taxable on trust income on the basis of dominion and control. The justification for including the trust income in the settlor's gross income must be found in these sections of the Code. Examination of the Code provisions discloses the following factors to be considered in determining whether the settlor has eliminated the trust income from his gross income:

1. Are there administrative powers retained by the settlor?

2. May the income or principal return to the settlor?

3. Is the income or principal of the trust used to discharge the settlor's legal obligations, including his obligation to support or maintain some dependent or other person?

4. Is the income or principal of the trust to be used for paying premiums on the settlor's life insurance policies?

5. If there is a power to control beneficial enjoyment, though no benefit may be conferred upon the settlor, is this power in the settlor, in a subordinate party, in an independent party, or in an adverse party?

6. If there is a power to control beneficial enjoyment, though no benefit may be conferred upon the settlor, does the power relate to income only, or to principal only, or to both income and principal?

7. If there is a power to control beneficial en-

joyment, though no benefit may be conferred upon the settlor, is the power extensive or limited as to the variation in beneficial enjoyment?

In conclusion, caution is in order for anyone planning the use of trusts in estate arrangements. It is essential that strict compliance be made with the rules set forth in the Code in order to obtain the desired result of the planning effort. However, even though there is generally no federal tax advantage to the revocable trust, it is especially suited for one not financially able to irrevocably part with portions of his property during life.

Miscellaneous Types of Trusts

A *reciprocal,* or *cross-trust,* doctrine is a judicial concept that switches grantors of trusts in order to prevent tax avoidance. Suppose Baker creates a trust for the benefit of Carl, and Carl also sets up a trust of equal value for Baker. Under the terms of Baker's trust, any income is paid to Carl for life with the remainder to Carl's children. Similarly, the trust created by Carl provides for income to Baker for life with the remainder to Baker's children. This is not a tax-planning technique even though technically neither grantor has retained a life estate. The courts use the reciprocal trust doctrine in order to switch the grantors of the trusts. Each grantor is treated as if he created a trust under which he retains a life interest, and thereby the trust assets are included in his gross estate under Section 2036 as a retained life estate.[14]

The *apocalypse trust* is also meeting opposition from the IRS. Under such an arrangement a taxpayer transfers to a trust all his assets and assigns his lifetime services to the trust. For example, a doctor or dentist may transfer his place of business to a trust. The beneficiaries are generally the taxpayer's family, with the grantor retaining broad powers over the income and corpus of the trust. The trust collects all the taxpayer's income and deducts all the taxpayer's expenses. The purpose of this arrangement is to shift income to taxpayers in lower-tax brackets as well as to avoid the estate tax. Four revenue rulings bar the use of these apocalypse trusts.[15]

USES OF TRUSTS IN ESTATE PLANNING

Although several uses and advantages of trusts were given in other parts of this chapter, this section illustrates a few specific examples where trusts can be put to good use in estate planning. Of course, any time that a trust is devised for any estate-planning program, that trust must be tailored to meet the needs and circumstances applicable to the specific situation. The illustrations given here will be generalized situations, and therefore, the trusts suggested are not designed to solve specific problems.

Generation Skipping

Estate owners often wish to avoid having to pay estate taxes on successive life estates. Many times the estate owner will be satisfied to skip the tax at the death of his primary beneficiary. Skipping the estate tax on the death of the primary beneficiary can be accomplished by the use of a trust. The estate owner simply leaves his estate in trust, with the income going to his/her spouse for life and the remainder to the children upon the death of the remaining spouse. There is no estate tax on the property in which survivor merely held a life interest.

The Tax Reform Act of 1976 took away some of the estate tax advantages of a long-term trust. Specifically, the law imposes an estate tax on generation-skipping trusts. A generation-skipping trust is a trust in which the taxpayer passes property to a person at least two generations younger, but some control or benefits of the property first go to some individual of the in-between generation.

The generation-skipping tax is triggered when there is termination of the benefits to the in-between generation or when there is a distribution of trust corpus to the ultimate beneficiary. Even though this new generation-skipping tax is imposed upon the trust corpus, it is computed as if the individual in the in-between generation owned the property outright. The applicable tax (sometimes called Chapter 13 tax) is essentially equivalent to the transfer tax that would have been imposed if the assets actually had been transferred outright to each successive generation that had beneficial enjoyment or control over the assets. Although the amount of the tax is calculated with reference to the "deemed transferor's" marginal tax rate, the actual tax is payable generally *from the trust property* and not from the property of the intermediate beneficiary's estate.

There is one important exclusion to the generation-skipping tax. This exclusion occurs in the very common case in which the taxpayer leaves the income of a trust to his/her children and the remainder to grandchildren. Such a generation-skipping transfer to the taxpayer's grandchildren receives an exclusion to the tax in the amount of $250,000 of trust corpus per child (not grandchild) of the taxpayer.

Notice that this exclusion is applied to the aggregate *fair market value* of the trust property upon the termination of the grantor-children's life income interest in the trust. Therefore, since the grantor is unable to predict the appreciation in the assets or an overall inflation level, tax planning is difficult in this area.

One way to avoid the generation-skipping tax is to "layer" gifts so as to completely skip the grantor's children by giving them some assets outright and placing approximately $250,000 *per child* in generation-skipping trusts. Another way is to place property in trusts for *grandchildren* without any life estate for children.

The generation-skipping tax must now be considered when dealing with most trust transfers. Certain transfers still avoid the generation-skipping tax. For example, an individual can transfer income-producing property to a trust, income to his spouse for life, and at her death the corpus could be distributed as follows:

1. To the children in equal shares.
2. If any child is not alive, such share goes to the child's surviving issue.
3. If such nonliving child has no surviving issue, the share goes to the individual's surviving issue.

In any one of these three situations, there would be no generation-skipping tax.

Consider another example. An individual transfers income-producing property to a trust, income to his wife for life, and at her death the trust corpus is to be divided into equal shares for his children, each child to receive the income from his/her share for life, and at the child's death, the corpus to be distributed as follows:

1. Child's share at death to be distributed to his/her surviving issue.
2. If the child has no surviving issue, his/her share is to be allocated among the individual's surviving issues:
   (a) Any share of a child is to be added to his/her trust.
   (b) The share of any other issue is to be distributed to him/her.

There is no generation-skipping tax at the death of the wife who possesses an income interest. However, when a child dies with a distribution of corpus to his/her children (or the children of his/her siblings) the so-called Chapter 13 tax would apply to the excess of the total *value* of the distributions over $250,000. There is no tax on the portion of the decedent's trust share added to the trust shares of the decedent's siblings.

Avoiding Probate

Many estate owners dislike the fact that the amount of their estate and the way in which they provide for their family become a public record. All property subject to probate or to court disposition becomes public record, and thus is open to public scrutiny. The sure way to avoid this public scrutiny is to avoid probate.

The estate owner can avoid probate by placing his property in a trust for the benefit of his/her survivors. The trust may be either an *inter vivos* trust or a testamentary trust. The fact is that property left in trust is not subject to probate; neither does it become part of the basis from which the executor's and attorney's fees are determined. Thus, by placing the property in trust, the estate owner avoids the public scrutiny and reduces the amount of the executor's fees that this estate would have to pay. Also, disgruntled relatives are more prone to attack the capacity of the estate owner to make a will than his right to establish an *inter vivos* trust.

Continuance of Management

As already pointed out earlier in this chapter, the trust is very advantageous where continuous, competent management of the trust property is necessary. In some cases the estate owner may be aging and may doubt his own future ability to make the proper decisions. Another situation where the trust is beneficial is where there is a need to achieve a continuing and unified management of the property so that it will be uninterrupted by the death of the estate owner. Such flexibility is especially important when the trust property is a going concern and the estate owner does not have survivors capable of or interested in taking over the business. Even if the trust property is not a going concern, the estate owner may wish to provide competent management of such property for the benefit of his heirs. All these types of situations can easily be handled with a properly drawn trust.

Certainly there are many cases in which the estate owner has a surviving spouse or other beneficiary who has proved himself to be incapable of properly managing financial affairs. In such a situation the estate owner may establish a trust to support such a beneficiary; the most common type of trust used for this purpose is the *spendthrift* trust. Of course the estate owner may simply want to provide for the health, education, and other needs of a minor child. Support trusts, which were discussed earlier, are used to achieve these results.

Equally important is the need in many cases to withhold property from a person who is legally unable to manage his own affairs. These individuals include infants and persons who are mentally incompetent. The trust form is much better suited to practical administration in such cases than is a guardianship.

The estate owner can also secure income tax benefits through the use of trusts. If he makes an irrevocable trust, then the income from the trust property is not included in his gross income. If the estate owner cannot afford to part irrevocably with the property, he may transfer the property into a revocable trust for a period greater than ten years (the so-called Clifford trust), and the income from such trust will not be included in his gross income.

POWERS OF APPOINTMENT

Powers of appointment may be a useful estate-planning tool when setting up trusts. There are two types of powers: a general power of appointment and a special power of appointment. A person has a *general* power of appointment if (1) he can appoint the property to himself, (2) to his estate, (3) to his creditors, or (4) to creditors of his estate. Any other power is considered to be a *special* power of appointment (that is, the power to appoint to anyone except in the preceding four categories).

If a person has a *general* power of appointment, for estate and gift tax purposes he is treated as if he owns the property. If he exercises the general power during lifetime, he pays a gift tax. If he holds on to the power (dies without exercising it), the property is included in his gross estate. As a general rule, one should not give a general power of appointment.

Assume that Mr. Devour gives property to a trust, giving his grandson income for life, with a power to appoint to anyone except himself, his estate, his creditors, or his estate's creditors. The grandson could be given the power "to invade corpus in order to survive, to maintain himself, or to support himself." By giving the grandson a *special* power of appointment, the grandson could defer the generation-skipping tax by exercising the special power to create a present interest in a beneficiary in the same generation as the grandson (that is, grandson's spouse). If a grandson had been given a general power of appointment, there would be a tax on the grandson's death.

The estate planning could go a step further. Grandson could be given the power to invade corpus on December 31 of each year to the extent of $5,000 or 5 percent of the corpus (whichever is greater). This is a contingency distribution and would be taxed only if the donor dies *on* December 31 (which is unlikely if you know the doctor).

Often in a marital trust, the trustees have the discretionary power to invade principal in favor of the surviving spouse for her well-being, maintenance, and health (that is, an ascertainable standard). Where the marital trust and the residuary trust are quite wealthy, it may be advisable to provide the surviving spouse with enough flexibility to invade the corpus of the marital trust in order to allow lifetime gifts to other family members. Remember that the principal of the marital trust is included in the surviving spouse's estate because of her testamentary power of appointment; thus, reduction of the value of the trust's principal through lifetime gifts may be wise.

There is an unlimited number of uses of trusts designed to meet the needs of special situations. Of course it is not feasible or even possible to list or discuss everyone of these. The illustrations discussed above were presented to give the reader some insight into the many uses and advantages of trusts in estate planning.

CONCLUSION

The flexibility and benefits of both the *inter vivos* and testamentary trusts make them one of the most effective tools of estate planning. A properly conceived trust, drawn with due regard for economic and family considerations as well as tax benefits, can insulate trust property from estate tax and prevent unnecessary attribution of trust income.

When a trust is established, it is natural and proper that the settlor and his advisers plan it in such a way as to obtain the most favorable tax consequences. But the purpose of its establishment is ordinarily not just to save taxes; these are incidental, if they can be at all, to other elements in the process of carrying out the strong social and economic purposes of providing an orderly and sensible devolution of property.

Thus, there are many factors other than the tax advantages to consider before including a trust in the estate plan. Consideration must be given to the economic and social needs of the proposed beneficiaries of the trust, and it must be determined that the trust can reasonably satisfy these needs. The trust and the results of its operation must be evaluated in the light of the overall objectives of the estate owner. If the trust is to be implemented, it must help achieve the objectives of the estate owner rather than hinder the achievement of those objectives. Also, an evaluation must be made of the management of the trust property; that is, the ability and accomplishments of the trustee must be considered.

REFERENCES

1. George C. Bogert and George T. Bogert, *The Law of Trusts and Trustees*, 2d ed. (St. Paul, Minn.: West Publishing Co., 1965), sec. 1.
2. American Law Institute, *Restatement of the Law, Second, Trusts*, 2d ed. (St. Paul, Minn.: American Law Institute Publishers, 1959), sec. 368.
3. George C. Bogert, *Handbook of the Law of Trusts*, 4th ed. (St. Paul, Minn.: West Publishing Co., 1963), p. 142.

4. *Richard I. Armantrout et al.*, 67 T.C. No. 82 (1977); Rev. Rul. 75-448.
5. Edwin H. Corbin, "Living Trusts in Action," *Trusts and Estates*, CVI (July, 1967), p. 625.
6. *Ibid.*, p. 627.
7. A. James Casner, *Estate Planning*, Vol. 1, 3d ed. (Boston: Little, Brown, and Company, 1961), p. 94.
8. *American Law Reports Annotated*, LXIV (Rochester, N.Y.: The Lawyers Co-Operative Publishing Company, 1929), p. 466; *American Law Reports Annotated Second Series*, XLIV (Rochester, N.Y.: The Lawyers Co-Operative Publishing Company, 1956), p. 521.
9. William Schwartz, *Future Interest and Estate Planning.* (Cincinnati: The W. H. Anderson Company, 1965), pp. 86–87.
10. Section 677(b); see *Morrill* v. *U.S.*, 228 F. Supp. 734 (D.Me. 1964).
11. Section 673(c).
12. Gilbert Thomas Stephenson, *Estates and Trusts*, 4th ed. (New York: Appleton-Century-Crofts, Inc., 1965), pp. 102–103.
13. *Ibid.*, p. 329.
14. *U.S.* v. *Grace*, 395 U.S. 316 (1969).
15. Rev. Rul. 75-257 through Rev. Rul. 75-260.

9

Philanthropy in Your Estate Plan

What always happens—what has happened in every na-
tion that has ever set up a graduated income tax—is that
the highest *actual* rates are paid by the middle class.
From *The April Game*

MOTIVATED by social or moral reasons, many individuals combine tax savings with philanthropy.
Gifts to charitable organizations can be made during
lifetime or at death through a will. This chapter is
devoted exclusively to the restrictions on such contributions and to significant tax savings that can result from properly planned transactions. Any estate
plan should consider the benefits of charitable giving.

HOW TO TREAT CONTRIBUTIONS

Lifetime contributions to certain qualified organizations are deductible from adjusted gross income (D from AGI) by taxpayers. Since they are D from AGI, taxpayers should make charitable contributions only in years in which they have enough itemized deductions to exceed their standard deduction; otherwise, the contributions are useless as tax savings. Among charitable organizations generally qualified as recipients are: a church or association of churches; a college or university; a hospital; governmental units; certain private foundations; a community chest, trust, fund, or foundation that is organized and operated exclusively for religious, charitable, scientific, literary, or educational purposes, or for the prevention of cruelty to children or animals; and other organizations that are exempted from taxation under Section 501(a) of the Internal Revenue Code.

Details of specific, national, nonprofit charities may be obtained by writing to the Solicitation Review Manager, Council of Better Business Bureaus, 1150 Seventeenth Street, N.W., Washington, D.C. 20036. For local charities, consult with the Chamber of Commerce or Better Business Bureau. Keep in mind that lifetime charitable gifts reduce one's estate, which in turn reduces the estate tax.

In order to appreciate the limitations on lifetime charitable contributions, one must understand that there are two types of charitable organizations: the public charity and the private charity. Gifts to public charities qualify for a 50 percent ceiling; that is, an individual can deduct up to 50 percent of his "contribution base." Those contributions in excess of this ceiling can be carried over for the next five tax years. A person's "contribution base" is his/her adjusted gross income, disregarding any net operating-loss carry back. The charities qualifying for the 50 percent ceiling include most churches, American Red Cross, American Philatelic Society, American Numismatic Association, Boy Scouts, Girl Scouts, Ford Foundation, and many other well-known charities. When in doubt, ask the potential charitable organizations if contributions to them qualify for a deduction.

All other qualified charities that are not 50 percent charities are 20 percent charities such as private foundations or organizations (for example, Crumbley and Milam Foundation). Gifts to these charities are deductible up to the lesser of 20 percent of the taxpayer's contribution base, *or* 50 percent of his contribution base *minus* contributions to 50 percent charities (including carry-overs of such contributions, and no reduction for the 30 percent ceiling on appreciated property). For example, if you contribute 38 percent of your contribution base to a 50 percent charity (say, a church), your contributions to 20 percent charities are deductible only up to 12 percent of your contribution base. Furthermore, you are *not* allowed to carry over any excess gifts to 20 percent charities.

An individual whose business is operated as a corporate organization may also have the corporation make charitable gifts. A corporation is allowed to deduct charitable contributions up to 5 percent of its taxable income per year. An excess contribution in any one year may be carried over and is deductible prorated for each of the five succeeding tax years. If the corporation is in the 48 percent tax bracket, approximately one-half of any contribution is, in effect, contributed by the federal government.

TAX SAVINGS FROM LIFETIME CONTRIBUTION

The computation of tax saving from lifetime giving by an individual is a little more complicated, but the Institute of Business Planning, Inc., in New York City has simplified the process somewhat by providing the accompanying table to determine the saving per $100 of deductible charitable contributions. The figures are based on the allowance of a full deduction for the entire value of the gift.

If taxable income before deducting contribution is:	Saving per $100 of deductible charitable contribution is:		
	For single persons	For married persons filing jointly	For heads of households
$ 10,000	$25	$22	$23
12,000	27	22	25
16,000	31	25	28
22,000	38	32	35
30,000	45	39	42
50,000	60	50	55
60,000	62	53	58
80,000	66	58	62
100,000	69	60	64

Ordinary Income-Type Property

Three sets of tax rules apply to all contributions of appreciated property (that is, all property that would give rise to any gain if sold, such as diamonds, rare coins or stamps, antiques, and jewelry):

1. Ordinary income-type property.
2. Tangible personal capital-gain property, and contributions of capital-gain property to certain private foundations.
3. Appreciated capital-gain property.

Property appreciation that would not be *all* long-term capital gain to the contributor if he sold it at its fair market value on the date it was contributed falls into this first category of ordinary income-type property. For a charitable contribution of any property that gives rise to an ordinary income appreciation on disposition, the property's fair market value is reduced by the amount of the ordinary income appreciation in order to determine the deductible amount. For example, Larry purchased a painting for $2,500 and contributed it to a museum four months later when it was worth $4,000. Since the $1,500 of appreciation is short-term gain, Larry's charitable deduction is only $2,500 ($4,000 − $1,500).

If a dealer gives assets from his/her inventory to a charity, such property falls within this first category. That is, if the assets are sold from inventory, any income would be ordinary income. This is the critical question as to whether an individual is a dealer or a nondealer. A person who is *not* a dealer must take care to avoid this dealer "taint." Too many transactions may too often cause an IRS agent to classify an individual as a dealer; then any gains on the contribution of property would be ordinary income rather than capital gain.

Obviously, an individual should avoid gifts of short-term and ordinary income property to charities whenever possible. Such property should be donated to a charity in a will in order to obtain a full estate tax deduction. Or he/she may wish to leave ordinary income property in a will to his children, who will possibly get a fresh-start stepped-up-basis for appreciation occurring before 1977; they can then give the property to a charity and obtain a full income tax deduction.

Tangible Personal Capital Gain Property

A second category of appreciated property involves the contribution of tangible, personal, capital gain property. As a general rule, such property receives a full deduction. Capital gain property is a capital asset, and if sold at the time contributed will result in a long-term capital gain. A rare coin or stamp collection held by a collector or investor for at least nine months (12 months after 1977) and one day falls within this definition of capital gain property. However, a coin or stamp collection in the inventory of a dealer would not fall within this definition, but would be considered to be ordinary income property.

Two exceptions apply to this second category. First, if the asset contributed is tangible personal property, then in order to qualify for the full deduction, its utilization by the charity must be *directly related to the exempt function of the charity.* If not directly related to the exempt function of the charity, then the deduction is limited to cost *plus* 50 percent of the appreciation. For example, Jerry purchases a stamp collection for $2,500, holds it for 18 months, and then contributes it to a church when it is worth $4,000. The church sells it. Since the stamps are *not* directly related to the exempt function of the church, the deduction would be limited to Jerry's cost of purchase plus one-half of the appreciation, $750—a total deduction of $3,250. However, if the stamps were donated to a museum to be used for display purposes, Jerry would be entitled to the larger $4,000 deduction.

Thus, whether a contribution is for an "unrelated use" or "directly related use" by a charity is very important to a taxpayer. The term "unrelated use" means a use unrelated to the purpose or function constituting the exemption tax basis of the charitable organization. For example, if a rare gem collection contributed to an educational institution is used for educational purposes by placing it in a library for display and study by students, the use is not an unrelated use. But if the collection is sold and the proceeds are used by the organization for educational purposes, the use of the property is an "unrelated use." If a gem collection is contributed to a charitable organization or governmental unit, the use of the collection is not an "unrelated use" if the donee sells or otherwise disposes of an insubstantial portion of the collection. Obviously, potential donors of appreciated tangible personal property must match the item of property to the appropriate charity. For example, rare coins should be given to the American Numismatic Association, rare stamps to the American Philatelic Society, and so forth.

Maintenance of Proof

What proof of use should the taxpayer maintain? First, he may establish that the property is not in fact put to an unrelated use by the charity. Or second, at the time of the contribution it is reasonable to anticipate that the property will *not* be put to an unrelated use by the charity. In the case of a gift of property to a museum, if the donated property is of a general type normally retained by the museum, it is reasonable for the taxpayer to anticipate (unless he has actual knowledge to the contrary) that the property will *not* be put to an unrelated use, regardless of whether it is later sold or exchanged with another museum.

If a taxpayer makes a charitable contribution of appreciated artistic articles (for example, antiques, etchings, furs, jewelry) and claims a deduction in excess of $200, he must attach to his income tax return the following information:

1. Name and address of the organization to which the contribution was made.
2. The date of the actual contribution.
3. A detailed description of the property (such as coins or stamps) and its condition.
4. The manner of acquisition (by purchase, gift, inheritance, or other means).
5. The fair market value of the property along with the method utilized in determining the fair market value. If there was an appraisal, a copy of the signed report of the appraiser should be provided.

6. The cost or adjusted basis of the property.
7. Where the deduction is reduced by any of the appreciation, the reduced amount.
8. Any agreement or understanding between the taxpayer and the charity.
9. The total amount claimed as a deduction for the tax year.

Any deduction for a charitable contribution must be substantiated, when required by the District Director, by a statement from the organization to which the contribution was made. This statement should indicate whether the organization is a domestic organization, the name and address of the contributor, the amount of the contribution, the date of actual receipt of the contribution, and whatever additional information the District Director may deem necessary. When the property has a fair market value in excess of $200 at the time of receipt, the statement should also indicate the location of each item, if it is retained by the organization, the amount received by the organization on any sale of the property, the date of sale, or, in case of disposition other than sale, the method of disposition. The statement should indicate the use of the property by the organization and whether or not it is used for a purpose or function constituting the basis for the charity's exemption from income tax under Internal Revenue Code Section 501 or, in the case of a governmental unit, whether or not it is used exclusively for public purposes.

Gifts to Private Foundations

A second type of transaction causes a one-half reduction in the appreciation of the contributed property. If capital gain property is given to a private foundation (which is *not* a private operating foundation or community foundation), and the donor does not make qualifying distributions equal to the amount of such contributions within 2½ months after the close of the year, then the deduction is limited to the property's fair market value *minus* one-half of the appreciation.

Appreciated Capital Gain Property

A third category of appreciated property involves the contribution of appreciated capital gain property to a charity which is directly related to an exempt function. Capital gain property is a capital asset and, if sold at the time contributed, gives rise only to long-term capital gain. Diamonds or gems, rare coins or stamps, antiques, and similar items qualify as capital assets, and, if sold at the time contributed, give rise only to long-term capital gain. Such items qualify as capital gain property. When a taxpayer contributes appreciated capital gain property to a qualified charity, his deduction ceiling is reduced to 30 percent rather than the normal 50 percent, *unless* the taxpayer makes a special election to reduce the amount of this contribution.

In other words, the total amount of contribution of capital gain property considered for deduction purposes for any tax year cannot exceed 30 percent of the taxpayer's contribution base (generally adjusted gross income). When an individual makes a special election, his deduction ceiling remains at 50 percent along with a 50 percent carry-over, but the taxpayer may deduct only the basis of the capital gain property *plus* one-half of any appreciation.

For example, assume that Chuck Charitable, who has a $10,000 adjusted gross income, makes a charitable contribution during 19X7 of part of his rare stamp collection to the American Philatelic Society for display purposes. The portion of the collection contributed has a basis of $2,000, but is valued at $10,000 on the date of contribution. Under the general rule, he has made a contribution of $10,000. During 19X7 Chuck may deduct $3,000 (30% × $10,000) and have a contribution carry-over of $7,000 (but subject to the 30 percent carry-over rule).

On the other hand, if Chuck so desires, he may *elect* to value his contribution at $6,000 ($2,000 basis plus 50 percent of $8,000 appreciation). In this case, he could deduct $5,000 during 19X7 (50% × $10,000) with a contribution carry-over of $1,000 (subject to the 50 percent carry-over rule). A taxpayer probably will not wish to elect the 50 percent rule when he makes a contribution of highly appreciated property.

Of course, a taxpayer who owns property that is worth substantially less than its cost basis should sell it and then contribute the proceeds to the charity.

If a person contributes his property to a charitable organization and pays an appraisal fee to a dealer in order to determine the fair market value of the property, the appraisal expenses are deductible from his adjusted gross income, provided he itemizes his deductions and does not use the standard deduction.

Bargain Sale of Property

A bargain sale may be an excellent technique to minimize a donor's out-of-pocket cost. Before the law was changed in 1969, a taxpayer could sell appreciated property at cost to a charity and end up with his investment back without any tax plus a charitable deduction for the appreciation. Now, however, he must allocate his cost basis between the part of the property that he sold and the part that is a gift. Presto! He has a taxable gain on the bargain sale, but he still has *minimized the out-of-pocket cost of his charitable gift*. On the other hand, if a donor wishes to give the charity the largest benefit, he should make an ordinary gift to his selected charity.

For example, Cherry Charitable sells her rare coin collection worth $10,000 (which has been held a number of years) to a museum for her cost of $4,000. She must allocate 60 percent of her cost ($2,400) to the portion given and 40 percent ($1,600) to the portion sold. If she is in the 50 percent tax bracket, her $6,000 gift ($10,000 − $4,000) saves her $3,000 in taxes, and she recovers her $4,000 investment—a nice total of $7,000. If we assume further that she does not have capital gains in excess of $50,000, she will pay a tax of no more than $600 on her $2,400 ($4,000 − $1,600) long-term capital gain (25% × $2,400). Her net return is thus $6,400 and her favorite charity has $6,000 more in its coffers.

Suppose Cherry makes an outright gift of the coins to the museum. If the coins are directly related to the exempt function of the museum, the

$10,000 gift saves her $5,000, and the museum gets the full $10,000 tax basis.

Contribution of Services

No deduction is allowed for the contribution of services. For example, suppose you donate your services to the nonprofit Girl Scouts organization. The cost of your time is not deductible. However, unreimbursed expenditures such as transportation or lodging made incidental to the rendering of services to a qualified organization are deductible as contributions. The standard mileage rate for computing the cost of operating an automobile in rendering this service is seven cents per mile. Parking fees and tolls are deductible in addition to this mileage allowance.

Future Interest

A transfer of a future interest in property to a qualified charity may *not* be deducted as a charitable contribution until all intervening interest in, and rights to, the possession or enjoyment of the property have expired. Thus, except for a remainder interest in a residence or farm and certain remainder interest in a trust, no deduction is allowed for a gift in the future. Suppose an individual conveys by deed of gift to a museum the title to a gem collection in 19X7, but reserves the right to the use, possession, and enjoyment of the collection during his/her lifetime. At the time of the gift, the value of the gem collection is $40,000. Since the contribution consists of a future interest in tangible personal property in which the taxpayer has retained an intervening interest, no contribution is considered to have been made in 19X7. Assume that the taxpayer relinquishes all right to the use, possession, and enjoyment of the gem collection, and delivers it to the museum in 19X8 when the collection is worth $45,000. In this case the taxpayer is treated as having made a charitable contribution of $45,000 in 19X8.

Where a charitable gift exceeds $3,000 *or* is a future-interest gift, the transfer must eventually be reported on a gift tax return.

But when the charitable gift is reported, the taxpayer is allowed a deduction *on the gift tax return* (that is, a "wash" effect). There is no percentage limitation as to the amount deductible on the gift tax return. A donor is not forced to file on a quarterly basis the value of qualified charitable transfers. Instead, he/she is allowed to report the charitable transfers on the fourth-quarter return, *or* at an earlier time if required to file a return for a noncharitable gift.

A deduction is allowed on the federal estate tax return for any bequests, legacies, devises, or transfers to a charitable organization or unit of government at the decedent's death. This deduction is more fully discussed in Chapter 6.

10

Compensation and Estate Planning

Nothing is easier than the expenditure of public money.
It doesn't appear to belong to anyone.
The temptation is overwhelmingly
to bestow it on somebody.
Calvin Coolidge

CORPORATE executives are likely to be compensated in various ways. Compensation plans range from current salary to death-benefit-only plans. Since these various forms of executive compensation are significantly different, an executive must evaluate not only the economic impact of his/her compensation plan, but also the income and estate tax ramifications.

Before considering the estate tax consequences and estate-planning avenues involving compensation, a brief review of the income tax considerations is necessary.

INCOME TAXATION OF COMPENSATION

Salaries, commissions, and bonuses are taxed to the cash basis taxpayer in the year he receives such payment. Even though such types of compensation leave little room for tax planning, Section 1348 provides that such earned income is taxed at a maximum rate of 50 percent. In many situations, this maximum tax of 50 percent, along with the high rate of inflation, enhances the desirability of taking compensation in the form of current cash payments.

Retirement Plans

Since the enactment of the Pension Reform Act of 1974 (ERISA) and all its many requirements, a large number of corporations have dropped their qualified retirement plans. These employers as well as many others have turned to nonqualified plans that can be discriminatory and do not have to meet any special statutory provisions. Nonqualified plans may take any number of forms. For instance, the plan may be funded or unfunded, an employee trust may or may not be set up, or the plan may simply state that payments will be made in the future. These payments or the amounts thereof may or may not be based upon future events, continued service by the employee, or other conditions, and some nonqualified plans may be purely voluntary arrangements.

The income tax consequences of nonqualified plans depend upon the nature, type, and conditions of the plan and are governed by Section 83. If the plan is funded and the employee is given immediate rights that are not subject to risks, the employee must include in his gross income each year the amount of contributions made by the employer on his account. However, if the employee's rights are subject to a substantial risk of forfeiture (SRF), he has no immediate income or income tax; but in the year in which his rights become nonforfeitable (vested) or the SRF lapses, the entire value of his interest in the fund must be included in his income for tax purposes. If the employee is required to perform future services as a condition of vesting, his rights are deemed to be subject to a substantial risk of forfeiture.

If the nonqualified plan is unfunded, the employee has no income for tax purposes until the year in which funds are actually or constructively received by him. Constructive receipt of funds, discussed later in this chapter, has been the downfall of many taxpayers. The taxpayer should carefully avoid the pitfalls of constructive receipt. Revenue Rule 60-31 gives some insight in determining what types of deferred compensation will or will not be treated as constructively received.

Even with all the additional requirements and restrictions imposed by ERISA, qualified pension and profit-sharing plans continue to be two of the primary types of executive compensation. The popularity of the plans may be traced to their favored tax treatment. The employer gets an immediate tax deduction for contributions made to the plan, but the employee is not taxed until he actually receives the benefits (or they are "made available" to him). For this purpose, "made available has the same meaning as constructively received." The tax treatment then depends upon whether the employee elects to take the benefits in a lump sum or in an annuity.

ANNUITY DISTRIBUTION

If the employee elects to take the benefits in annuity form, the benefits received are taxed in accordance with Section 72.[1] Section 72 provides for the computation of an exclusion ratio. This exclusion ratio is applied to all benefits received by the employee, and the ratio determines the amount of the benefit that can be excluded from income for income tax purposes. The remainder of each payment must be included in the taxpayer's gross income. The exclusion ratio is determined by dividing the employee's cost (if any) by the employee's expected return under the annuity contract. The taxpayer's expected return is generally found by multiplying the amount of the annual payment under the contract by the proper multiple, which is determined by using the actuarial tables prescribed in Section 72 of the regulations. The multiple is basically the estimated life of the individual. Once the exclusion ratio is computed, it remains constant regardless of the time period for which the payments are made.

There is one major exception to Section 72 rules. If the employee will recover all his cost in the plan within the first three years, no exclusion ratio is computed. Instead, the taxpayer excludes all benefits from his gross income until he has fully recovered his cost. From that point, 100 percent of the additional benefits received are included in his gross income. Of course, if the employee has made no contributions to the plan, all payments received by him are included 100 percent in his gross income for income tax purposes.

PROFIT-SHARING PLANS

If an employee elects to receive a lump-sum distribution from a qualified plan, he has entirely different income tax consequences. The income taxation of lump-sum distribution was changed by the enactment of ERISA in 1973. Basically, the distribution is divided into two portions: a capital gain portion and an ordinary income portion. The capital gain portion is attributable to pre-1974 contributions, and the ordinary income portion is attributable to post-1973 contributions. The ordinary income portion is determined this way:

$$\left.\begin{matrix} \text{Taxable amount} \\ \text{of distribution} \end{matrix}\right\} \times \left\{ \frac{\begin{matrix} \text{calendar years of participation} \\ \text{after 1973} \end{matrix}}{\begin{matrix} \text{total calendar years} \\ \text{of participation} \end{matrix}} \right.$$

The remainder of the distribution may be treated as a long-term capital gain. However, after the Tax Reform Act of 1976, one-half of any long-term capital gain is subjected to a higher minimum tax of 15 percent. In addition, ERISA provides a ten-year-forward averaging rule for the ordinary income portion that can be elected for the entire distribution. The ten-year-forward averaging rule is quite complicated and beyond the scope of this book, but the authors strongly recommend that all executive employees seek competent professional advice in examining the tax consequences of lump-sum distributions versus annuities from qualified plans.

STOCK DISTRIBUTIONS

Another type of deferred compensation is payable in the form of restricted property, such as restricted stock. These restrictions are of various types, such as a requirement that the employee does not actually receive the stock or has to return the stock if an additional period of employment is not completed. Of course these restrictions usually prohibit the employee from selling the stock during this time period. Normally, an employee is taxed on the excess of the fair market value of the property over cost (if any) of that property in the first tax year that the property is either transferable or is not subject to a substantial risk of forfeiture. By definition, there is a substantial risk of forfeiture if the employee's right to the property is conditional on performing substantial future services.[2]

Stock options are still another form of executive compensation. Stock options basically fall into two groups: qualified and nonqualified. However, the 1976 Tax Reform Act eliminated any future use of qualified stock options, but any employee still holding an option, or stock acquired through such an option, may receive its tax benefits. When an employee exercises a qualified stock option, he/she does not recognize any taxable income.[3] In addition, if the stock is held for at least three years, the entire gain on the sale is treated as long-term capital gain.[4] If the stock is disposed of before three years, the gain on the transfer is ordinary income to the extent of the difference between the fair market value of the stock when the option was exercised and the employee's cost of the stock.[5] Any additional gain is treated as a capital gain.[6]

When an employee receives a nonqualified stock option, it is necessary to determine if the stock has a readily ascertainable value. A stock option is deemed to have such value if it is actively traded on an established market or meets other requirements specified in Reg. 1.421-6(c)(3). If the stock has a readily ascertainable value (that is, a warrant), the employee has taxable income to the extent of the difference in the value of the option and the amount (if any) paid for it.[7] If the option does *not* have a readily ascertainable value, the employee realizes no income upon receiving the option, but instead would have taxable income if the option is exercised. The amount of taxable income is the difference between the fair market value of the stock and the price paid for such stock.[8]

LIFE INSURANCE BENEFITS

From a tax viewpoint, life insurance is a desirable fringe benefit. If the company provides the employee with group-term insurance, there is no income to the employee unless the face value of the policy exceeds $50,000. When the face value exceeds $50,000, the employee must include in his/her gross income an amount that represents the cost of the insurance *in excess* of $50,000. However, this amount is determined according to tables prescribed in Reg. 1.79-3. The rates in these schedules are quite low and do not in any way represent the actual cost of the insurance. For example, the amount included in income for a $250,000 group-term policy for a 46-year-old employee would be only $960. Currently, there are some proposed regulations that would replace the old schedules with new premium rates that would more closely approach the actual cost of the insurance.

Types of insurance other than group term provided for the employee by the employer generate taxable income to the employee in the amount of the cost of the insurance.

Another advantage to life insurance is that proceeds paid to a beneficiary by reason of death do not constitute income for income tax purposes. There is one exception to this rule, and that is where the proceeds are paid in installments. In such a situation, the interest part of the payment is deemed to be taxable income. However, if the beneficiary is the spouse of the insured, he/she may exclude the interest up to a maximum of $1,000 per year.[9]

DEATH-BENEFIT-ONLY PLAN

Another form of executive compensation that recently has been gaining in popularity is the death-benefit-only plan. Under such a plan, the corporation usually agrees to pay some amount to the deceased employee's heirs or estate. Generally, there are no income consequences to the employee because at no time are any benefits received. At the time of distribution the beneficiary must include the payments in his/her gross income for income tax purposes. However, up to $5,000 may be excluded under Section 101(b). This exclusion applies only to amounts paid on account of the employee's death, and only if the employee had no vested rights in the payments before death. However, the exclusion would still apply to vested benefits paid under a qualified plan if the benefits were paid to the employee's beneficiary by a lump-sum distribution within one tax year.[10]

ESTATE TAXATION OF COMPENSATION

With respect to estate tax, the major Code sections that deal with retirement benefits include the following:

Section 2033. Property in which the decedent had an interest.
Section 2035. Transactions in contemplation of death.
Section 2036. Transfers with retained life estate.
Section 2037. Transfers taking effect at death.
Section 2038. Revocable transfers.
Section 2039. Annuities.

Therefore, in planning his/her estate, the executive must pay particular attention to these sections when making decisions concerning retirement plans and/or funds. The following pages outline some of the potential tax consequences and provide some tips for tax-planning devices.

Nonqualified Plans

If the executive employee is covered by a non-qualified plan, it is quite difficult to generalize as to the tax consequences because of the many variations that could exist in the plans. However, deferred compensation payable to the employee's estate is generally included in his gross estate under Section 2033. If the deferred compensation is payable to any other beneficiary, it is normally included in the gross estate under Section 2039. Section 2039 deals with annuities that are receivable by a beneficiary as a result of the beneficiary's surviving the taxpayer (decedent).

In order for Section 2039 to apply, *all* four of the following conditions must exist:

1. Decedent was receiving or had the right to receive payment.
2. The right to such payment was for the decedent's life or for a period not ascertainable without reference to his death.
3. The decedent contributed to the cost of the contract.
4. The beneficiary is entitled to the benefits by reason of surviving the decedent.[11]

In the case of a nonqualified plan, any contributions made to the plan by the employer are deemed to be contributed by the decedent employee, and thus condition 3 is met.

Once determined that an annuity is to be included in the gross estate, the value of the annuity is determined according to Section 2039(b). Basically, the value of the annuity included in the gross estate is determined by multiplying the value of the annuity by a fraction, in which the numerator is the amount of the purchase price contributed by the decedent and the denominator is the total cost of the annuity. Since the employer's contribution to a nonqualified annuity is attributable to the employee, usually this fraction is 100 percent. The value of the annuity is the fair market value of the annuity contract as of the date of the decedent's death, and is usually determined by the actuarial tables found in Reg. 20.2031-8 and Reg. 20.2031-10.

TAX-PLANNING TIPS FOR NONQUALIFIED PLANS

The executive who is covered by a nonqualified retirement plan can do little to shelter his/her benefits from taxation. One thing possible is to transfer all rights in the plan to an irrevocable trust for the surviving spouse, children, or other beneficiaries. If the beneficiary is the taxpayer's spouse, under the new law property can be transferred up to $100,000 without incurring any gift tax. For other beneficiaries it is doubtful that there would be much tax savings, since the amount of the gifts (less a $3,000 exclusion) are added back to the estate before computing the estate tax. Some tax savings would occur if the value of the property significantly appreciates prior to death.

Another possibility for tax savings exists. If the executive has withdrawn from the nonqualified plan all the benefits to which he/she is personally entitled prior to death, then any death benefit paid to the named beneficiary may be excluded.[12] For a more detailed discussion, see the discussion of the death-benefit-only plan in the previous section.

A word of caution is necessary. All nonqualified plans should be evaluated to insure that there are no clauses in the plan that would constitute constructive receipt by the employee.

Qualified Retirement Plans

The law provides favored tax treatment to qualified retirement plans. As discussed earlier in this chapter, the employee is not taxed on the employer's contributions until the benefits are received. In addition, there are estate tax advantages in the form of an exclusion from the gross estate for a portion of the death benefits paid to a qualified beneficiary under a qualified plan.

QUALIFICATION OF NAMED BENEFICIARY

Section 2039(c) provides for an exclusion from the employee-decedent's gross estate of annuities or other payments (other than lump-sum distributions) that are made to a named beneficiary other than the decedent's estate or executor. In order to qualify, these benefits must be paid under a qualified plan or annuity contract purchased for an employee by a tax-exempt school, publicly supported charity, or retired serviceman's family protection plan. This exclusion is limited to the portion of the benefits paid to a qualified beneficiary and which are attributable to the employer's contributions. The benefits attributable to the employee's contributions must be included in the estate. The Tax Reform Act of 1976 made a very important change in this exclusion. For employees dying after December 31, 1976, the benefits must be paid in some form other than a lump-sum distribution if the exclusion is to apply. Payments received by the beneficiary within one taxable year are deemed to be a lump-sum distribution.[13]

Even though Section 2039(c) provides an exclusion, this exclusion is limited by the regulations to the amounts of the payments that were not actually or constructively received by the employee-decedent prior to death. The doctrine of constructive receipt (mentioned in the first section of this chapter) is quite important for this provision. Of course the doctrine of constructive receipt refers to the employee's rights to or command over funds whether or not he actually enjoys or uses the funds.

CONSTRUCTIVE RECEIPT

The doctrine of constructive receipt is especially critical in the case of an employee who leaves the company and receives an annuity contract from a qualified plan. In most situations, such a distributed contract allows the employee to (1) immediately surrender the contract for cash; (2) convert it into an immediately payable annuity; (3) hold it until the annuity starting date, and then select one of the annuity options; or (4) hold the contract until death, with the benefits going to the employee's beneficiaries.[14] In at least one case, the courts have held that such options constituted constructive receipt of the funds by the employee; therefore, Section 2039(c) did not apply, and the entire value of the annuity contracts had to be included in the employee's gross estate.[15] Such findings are clearly inconsistent with the income tax ruling related to the deferral of income under contracts providing for lump-sum versus annuity-type elections. An option to change the form of payment should not alter the tax consequences of the deferred feature.[16]

However, the IRS in a recent ruling helped provide some limited guidelines in this area: Rev. Rul. 77-34 provides that if the plan places substantial restrictions or limitations on an employee's rights, these rights do not come under the doctrine of constructive receipt.

Consider the following example. Suppose a plan provides that any employee who makes withdrawal from the plan is suspended from participating in the plan for 12 months and no contributions are to be made on his/her behalf by the company. Such restrictions on employees prohibit the amounts subject to withdrawal from falling under the doctrine of constructive receipt, and therefore retain eligibility for exclusion under Section 2039(c).

DEFERMENT OF ANNUITY PAYMENTS

Another problem in the area of the Section 2039(c) exclusion often arises when a retired employee tries to defer the receipt of his annuity payments under a qualified plan. Since it is necessary for benefits to be paid by a qualified plan if the exclusion is to apply, the employee's beneficiaries must receive payment under a contract that meets the requirements of Section 401(a) (qualified plan trust).[17] In the *Silverman* case,[17] the Court ruled that to exclude the benefits under Section 2039(c), the contracts held by the employee would have had to have been surrendered for annuity contracts in accordance with the qualified plan.[18] From this case, one can generalize (rule of *Silverman*) that for the exclusion to apply, the annuity contract must comply with the restrictions and settlement options available under the qualified plan.[19]

Tax-Planning Tips for Qualified Plans

An executive who is participating in a qualified plan may normally withdraw benefits when he/she (1) reaches 59½ years, (2) is separated from service with the company, or (3) upon death. In addition, there are usually several methods of withdrawal, the majority of which have been discussed earlier in this chapter. Of course, the timing and method of withdrawal are quite important from a tax standpoint. Lump-sum withdrawals are eligible for the ten-year-forward averaging schedule discussed earlier, while annuities are taxed under Section 72. In many situations the executive must weigh the investment opportunities of the net-after-tax withdrawal of the lump-sum distribution against the potential income tax benefits of receiving the funds in the form of an annuity over time. Each individual should seek competent advice before exercising his options.

Under the Tax Reform Act of 1976, an employee may now elect to treat all his lump-sum withdrawals as ordinary income eligible for the ten-year-forward averaging rule. This tax-law change should certainly be considered because without this election the employee's lump-sum withdrawal, to the extent of contributions made prior to 1974, is deemed to be a capital gain. The paradox here is that one-half of this capital gain is subject to the significantly increased minimum tax. The minimum tax is at the rate of 15 percent of tax preferences, and in many cases the significant reduction in the minimum tax exemption to $10,000 is even more drastic.

In addition, another change in the Tax Reform

Act of 1976 also applies. The new law includes amounts received as deferred compensation, annuities, or pensions as personal service income, and therefore are eligible for the 50 percent maximum tax. However, if an employee elects a lump-sum distribution, one-half of the capital gain portion must be used to reduce his personal service income, which would otherwise be eligible for the maximum tax. An employee should consider all alternatives before electing a lump-sum withdrawal from his/her qualified retirement plan.

Rollover Retirement or Annuity Withdrawals

If the employee's qualified plan is terminated, or he elects a lump-sum withdrawal, taxation still can be avoided upon his withdrawal. This avoidance can be done by "rolling over" the employee's entire lump-sum withdrawal into an individual retirement account or annuity or into another qualified plan if the employee takes a new job. For such an election to qualify, it must be completed within 60 days of the distribution of the proceeds from the qualified plan. However, such a rollover does have some limitations. The distributions from the IRA account are not eligible for the ten-year-forward averaging rule or for capital gain treatment.

However, under the 1976 Tax Reform Act, the value of any annuity receivable for a period of more than 36 months by a named beneficiary other than the employee's estate is excluded from the employee's gross estate under Section 2039(e), just as if it were being paid under the qualified plan.

If the executive decides upon a lump-sum withdrawal, but does not anticipate any future need for the proceeds, he/she should consider the creation of an irrevocable *inter vivos* trust for the benefit of children or grandchildren. If the proceeds from his/her qualified plan are transferred into such a trust, the transfer becomes a taxable gift. Since such taxable gifts are added back to the estate before applying the estate tax, it is doubtful that such a transfer would reduce estate taxes unless the value of the property appreciates after the gift. However, the trust relieves the employee of paying income tax on the investment income, and of course the estate will be reduced by the amount of the accumulated income.

Selection of Annuity Disbursement

If the employee elects to receive benefits in the form of an annuity, there are still several decisions to make. He must decide if the annuity should be for life only, a period certain, or a joint and survivor annuity. In many cases this decision is an economic one rather than a tax-related decision. Of course, if the annuity is for life only, there are no benefits remaining to be included in his/her estate. If the employee outlives the period certain, there will be no remaining benefits. But if the employee dies before the end of the period, the remaining benefits are subject to estate tax unless they qualify for exclusion under Section 2039(c).

Choice of Beneficiary

If the employee has elected a joint and survivor annuity, he/she will want to make sure that the benefits remaining after death will be excluded from his/her gross estate under Section 2039(c). To accomplish this exclusion, the employee should name a beneficiary other than the estate. This beneficiary should be under no legal obligation to pay any debts or taxes on the estate; this is especially true if the named beneficiary is a trust.

The employee's choice of a beneficiary to the remaining benefits of his retirement plan has some other important tax consequences. First, potential problems arise when the employee's benefits passing to a spouse do not qualify for the marital deduction because these proceeds were excluded from the gross estate. Second, the value of the proceeds would increase the size of the spouse's estate and, if he/she already holds substantial assets, could create even greater estate tax problems. Unless the spouse remarries, there would be no marital deduction for his/her estate. To avoid such consequences, the employee could name a trust as the beneficiary and give the trustee the power to accumulate or distribute income (as well as a five or five power) * to the surviving spouse for life, with the remainder going to children or other heirs upon his/her death. Such action would prohibit the benefits from being taxed in the survivor's estate and would also qualify for the Section 2039(c) exclusion in the decedent's estate.

Tax Considerations

Another related problem in naming an irrevocable beneficiary in order to receive the benefits of a trust or survivorship of an annuity is that the

* The "five or five power" concept refers to the power of the beneficiary of a trust to withdraw annually $5,000 or 5 percent of the assets of the trust. See E. W. Turley, "The 'Five or Five Power': An Obscure Estate Planning Tool," *Washington and Lee Law Review*, Vol. 33, No. 3, pp. 701–715.

employee is deemed to have made a taxable gift in the amount of the value of the survivorship rights. However, the Tax Reform Act of 1976 limited the amount of the taxable gift to the portion of the value of the benefits attributable to the employee's contributions.[20] Thus, if all contributions to the plan have been made by the employer, there is not a taxable gift.

A nontax-related problem concerning joint and survivor annuities is worth mentioning. It is quite possible that such a contract does not end when the employee divorces and remarries. The first spouse is more likely to receive the benefits upon the employee's death. Therefore, if an employee anticipates divorce, some other form of annuity contract probably should be selected.

If at the time the annuity payments are to begin, the employee is still employed, or both spouses have substantial income from other sources, he/she should consider establishing a ten-year trust (the Clifford trust) for some member of the family (other than the spouse) who is in a lower-income tax bracket. Of course the employee would be deemed to have made a taxable gift upon the creation of the trust. But the income from the trust would not be taxed to the employee because the income would go to the designated family member and would not become a part of the employee's gross estate; therefore, indirectly, this would save estate tax.

Deferral of Benefits
If an employee does not elect a lump-sum distribution or an annuity for life only, the exclusion provided by Section 2039(c) should certainly be considered. Once retirement benefits are with-

drawn, the rights to the exclusion are lost. If the employee does not need the funds and the retirement plan permits the deferral of benefits until actual retirement, instead of normal retirement, such a deferral should be considered because his/her estate will still be entitled to the Section 2039(c) exclusion. However, the employee must also be cautious of the *Silverman* rule. In cases where the qualified plan provides the employee with an election under Section 401(a)(14) to defer the retirement benefits beyond normal retirement age, then the retirement benefits are still eligible for exclusion. Where the plan does provide such an election, then in order for the exclusion to apply, such election should be removed from the annuity contracts. Also, to insure that the employee does not lose the Section 2039(c) exclusion, the contract should not allow the employee to defer receipt of the benefits by failing to surrender the contract to the issuer at the annuity starting date.[21] In addition, the plans should provide substantial restrictions or limitations (as illustrated in Rev. Rul. 77-34) in order to avoid the employee's being confronted with the doctrine of constructive receipt. These last suggestions are not something an individual employee can accomplish for his/her own estate planning, but the employer should be made aware of the potential tax traps so that the plans can be modified to meet these constraints.

STOCK OPTIONS

Even though the Tax Reform Act of 1976 eliminated post-1976 qualified stock options, the executive-employee who holds pre-1977 options or even nonqualified stock options must be concerned about the estate tax consequences. Unfortunately, there are no provisions in the Code or regulations that grant special concessions to stock options. Therefore, all stock options (qualified and nonqualified) owned by the employee at his death are included in his gross estate under Section 2033. The options would be valued at their fair market value on date of death for estate tax purposes.

Since, under the terms of a qualified option, the employee cannot transfer such options, only a few things can be done in the way of estate planning. However, in the case of a nonqualified stock option, the employee might consider making a gift of the option. A gift of a stock option does have some disadvantages. First, when the transferee exercises the option, the employee must include in personal income for income tax purposes the difference between the fair market value of the stock on date of exercise and the price paid for such stock. Second, under the new law, the amount of any taxable gifts is added to the estate before applying the estate tax rates. However, any appreciation in value between the date of the gift and the date of the employee's death is successfully removed from his/her estate.

The making of a gift of stock options should be considered only in connection with the overall estate plan. Such gifts should not be undertaken without prior professional advice.

LIFE INSURANCE

Section 2042 controls the estate taxation of life insurance. This section provides that the gross estate shall include the value of all proceeds from life insurance (1) that is payable to the decedent's estate or for the benefit of his executor or estate, or (2) that is payable to any other beneficiary if the decedent possessed at his death *any* incidents of ownership exercisable either alone or in conjunction with any other person. Therefore, it is quite apparent that any insurance in which the corporate employee owns an interest is included in gross estate. In addition, the proceeds will be taxed in the estate if they are payable to the estate or to the executor or for the benefit of the estate, regardless of who owns the policy. Inclusion in the estate often occurs when least expected.

One problem area is the inclusion of the proceeds in the estate when they are paid to a named beneficiary, but are made available for the benefit of the estate. This often happens when the beneficiary is required to pay some of the debts or obligations, such as funeral expenses of the estate. Another problem area is where the insurance has been used as collateral for the decedent's debts; such use would automatically throw the proceeds into the decedent's estate.

Incidents of Ownership

If the proceeds of the life insurance policy are payable to a named beneficiary other than the estate, the employee-decedent must make sure that *no* incident of ownership is retained if the proceeds are to be excluded from the gross estate. "Incidents of ownership" are not limited to ownership in a strict legal sense, but also include the right to economic benefits of the insurance policy. Therefore, "incidents of ownership" include the right (1) to name or change the beneficiary, (2) to surrender or cancel the policy, (3) to assign the policy for a loan or to borrow against the cash-surrender value. Also, "incidents of ownership" include any reversionary interest, whether arising by the terms of the policy, a contract, or operation of law in the policy or the proceeds of the policy, but only if the employee-decedent's reversionary interest immediately before death exceeds 5 percent of the value of the policy.

Insurance in Trust

If a life insurance policy is held in trust and under the terms of the policy or trust the employee-decedent (either alone or in conjunction with someone else) has the right to change the beneficial interest in the proceeds or policy, such person is deemed to have an incident of ownership. Where the employee-decedent is the sole or controlling stockholder (control means more than 50 percent of voting power) and the corporation retains some economic benefits (such as the right to change the beneficiary), then if the proceeds are payable to anyone other than for the benefit of the corporation, the employee-decedent is deemed to have retained some incidents of ownership, and the proceeds are included in gross estate. If the corporation is directly or indirectly the beneficiary and therefore the net worth of the corporation is increased, the decedent is not deemed to have retained incidents of ownership. In addition to the types of "incidents of ownership," mentioned above, one must evaluate the applicable state laws, especially in community-property states, to insure that these laws do not convey incidents of ownership to the decedent.[22] In a recent case, the court decided that if the taxpayer's consent was needed to change a beneficiary, the taxpayer had incidents of ownership.[23]

Prior to Rev. Rul. 72-307 an employee was deemed to have retained some incidents of ownership of group term insurance simply because he could terminate his employment and the insurance would be canceled. Under current law an employee can give away *all* incidents of ownership in group term insurance if he/she can assign ownership of the policy, and (1) has a right to convert the policy to ordinary insurance, (2) has assigned all rights including the right to convert, and (3) state law allows such an assignment.[24]

ESTATE-PLANNING TIPS FOR LIFE INSURANCE PLANS

An employee can reduce his gross estate, and thus his taxable estate, by prohibiting the inclusion of life insurance proceeds in his estate. This exclusion may be accomplished by naming a beneficiary other than the taxpayer's estate or executor, and by divesting himself of all incidents of ownership. The taxpayer may make a completed gift of the life insurance policy to another member of his family. Under current law the value of such a taxable gift is added back to his gross estate. However, in most cases the value of a life insurance policy during the taxpayer's life is much less than the proceeds paid upon death. Therefore, the value of the gift after the $3,000 annual exclusion might be very small.

All estate owners should have a competent professional review of their entire estate planning before making such a beneficiary transfer. This review is important for many reasons. One is that in many situations the entire purpose of buying life insurance is either to help build the estate or to provide liquidity for the estate. The proceeds from the insurance are to be used to help pay funeral expenses, administration expenses, or death taxes. Without these proceeds, many estates would have to sell other assets to meet obligations. Another warning is appropriate. If the estate owner transfers the policy, but requires the beneficiary to pay some of the debts or other obligations of the estate, the proceeds will be included in the estate. Thus, a gift tax is paid on the transfer and an estate tax on the proceeds.

Another problem in irrevocable assignments of life insurance is that conditions and relationships change. For instance, the executive might irrevocably assign his/her spouse a life insurance policy, but years later the couple divorces. Then there is the case of secondary beneficiaries. A policy is assigned to the employee's spouse, and the spouse dies first. This may cause two problems. First, the spouse's will leaves the insurance to the employee, in which case the proceeds will have to be included again in his estate. Second, the spouse might leave the insurance policy to minor children. Normally in such a situation, the proceeds cannot be borrowed by the estate; therefore, these funds would not be available to the estate in any manner.

If after careful investigation and analyses it is determined that the employee-taxpayer should reduce his gross estate by irrevocably transferring life insurance, there are several avenues for such transfers. The transfer can be in the form of an outright gift, or the transfer may be in the form of a trust. If the transfer is in trust, extreme caution must be used in drafting the trust instrument and the naming of the trustee so as to insure that the taxpayer does not retain any incidents of ownership. Expert counsel should be sought for these transfers.

The employee might transfer ordinary life insurance, split-dollar insurance, or group-life insurance. Each of these types presents special problems, but usually it is easier to completely and irrevocably transfer ordinary life insurance.

With group-life policies, the IRS has recently provided means of assigning such policies. If the group policy is an optional policy that the employee can buy, the employee could allow an "applicant owner" (a specified relative such as a husband or wife) to obtain the coverage as the person insured. If the relative pays the premiums out of his/her separate funds, the proceeds are excluded from the employee's gross estate because neither the employee nor the estate had any incidents of ownership.[25]

If the group-term policy is paid for by the employee, there are more problems in its transfer. A recent IRS ruling indicates the tax consequences of transferring such a policy to a trust. According to the ruling, if the policy had been in effect for five years and had been transferred to an irrevocable trust, the proceeds would be paid to named beneficiaries. The ruling implied that there was no taxable gift at the time of the transfer because the employee's interest in such a policy had no ascertainable value. Any future premium payments made by the employer would be additional compensation (even if not taxable) to the employee, and thus the insured person would be making a gift of such compensation to the assignee. This gift would be treated as a gift of present interest and therefore eligible for the $3,000 annual exclusion.[26]

Obviously, there are many tax consequences to life insurance and the transfer of such policies. Life insurance should be considered in all estate plans if for no other reason than to provide liquidity. However, the authors recommend that careful study of the entire estate plan be made before making transfers of such policies.

Death-Benefit-Only Plans

If providing for the employee's spouse after death is one of the primary concerns (and it should be) in the estate planning, then the executive should consider the nonqualified death-benefit-only type of plan. A death-benefit-only plan provides for the corporate employer to pay a death benefit or a salary continuation to a named beneficiary or beneficiaries of the employee after his death. If such a plan is properly constructed, the employee can successfully have the proceeds excluded from his estate. This also provides benefits to heirs at no income tax cost to the employee.

For the proceeds to be excluded, several factors must be considered. First, the employee cannot be participating or entitled to participate in any other retirement or deferred compensation plan because the IRS will treat the separate plans as one. Therefore, the employee is entitled to benefits and must include the entire proceeds in his estate as an annuity under Section 2039.[27]

A second factor or condition is that the employee may not retain the right to change the beneficiary because it provides him with the power to alter, amend, revoke, or terminate the benefits, thereby making those benefits includable in his gross estate under Section 2038.[28]

The Tax Reform Act of 1976 introduced a third factor. This pertains to a legally enforceable contract between the corporation and the employee in which the corporation is required to make such payments. In such a contract, the employee-decedent probably is deemed to have made a transfer to the beneficiary during his lifetime.[29] Under such circumstances the proceeds of the plan are not included in the gross estate, but the value of the transfer at the time of the transfer is added back to the estate before computing the estate tax.

Still another factor to be considered is the possession of a reversionary interest in the proceeds by the employee. Such reversionary interest might exist in a clause such as "benefits payable to my spouse if she is living, otherwise to my estate." [30] Or if a secondary beneficiary is not named, such an interest might be determined under the 5 percent rule of Section 2037.

In addition to the factors mentioned above, the law states that the benefits are pulled back into the employee's estate if the plan is entered into within three years of death (under Section 2035; gifts in contemplation of death).[31]

TAX-PLANNING TIPS WITH DEATH-BENEFIT-ONLY PLAN

Certain death-benefit plans should be used only in those cases where the employee has substantial retirement funds other than from the corporate employer. This type of plan is used only to provide benefits to heirs after the employee's death. However, if such a plan is feasible, it can provide substantial estate tax savings because its benefits are excluded from the gross estate. Because the costs (giving up rights to other retirement plans of the employer) are so significant, the authors recommend that careful consideration be given to the entire estate plan and other assets available for retirement before entering into such a contract.

To insure that the proceeds of a death-benefit-only plan are excluded from the gross estate, the following conditions should be carefully observed:

1. The employee cannot receive *any* nonqualified deferred compensation or retirement benefits from the same employer.
2. The employee *cannot* retain the right to change the beneficiary.
3. The employee *cannot* retain a reversionary interest, that is, name secondary beneficiaries other than his estate.
4. The employee must *not* have died within three years of entering into the agreement.[32]

However, if there is no enforceable contract (the corporation is authorized only to make payment, or the corporation voluntarily makes payment) the three-years-of-death rule is not important.

CONCLUSIONS

There are many types and combinations of compensation packages. Only a few of the many types of compensation have been discussed in this chapter. However, from this limited discussion, it is apparent that each type of compensation has both income tax and estate tax consequences. In some instances, the employee must forgo income tax advantages to provide estate tax benefits, and vice versa. To the extent that the employee can control the type or types of compensation to which he/she is entitled, the authors recommend that a determined effort be made to integrate the income tax and estate tax consequences with the pure economics of the individual's situation in order to devise a comprehensive estate plan.

REFERENCES

1. Section 402(a).
2. Section 83(a), (c).
3. Section 421(a)(1).
4. Section 422; Reg. 1.422-1.
5. Section 422(c)(4); Reg. 1.422-1(b).
6. *Ibid.*
7. Reg. 1.421-6.
8. Reg. 1.421-6(d)(1).
9. Section 101(d)(1)(B).
10. Section 101(b).
11. Section 2039(a).
12. Reg. 20.2039-1(b)(2).
13. Section 402(e)4(A).
14. Richard B. Robinson, "How to Ensure Estate Tax Exclusion for Annuity Contracts Distributed From Qualified Plans," *Estate Planning* (July 1977), p. 268.
15. *Northern Trust Company*, 389 F.2d 731, 21AFTR 2d 1615 (CA-7 1968).
16. For a more thorough discussion of this topic, see Robinson, *op. cit.*, 268–272.
17. *Estate of Silverman.* 61 T.C. 605 (1974).
18. *Ibid.*

19. Robinson, *op. cit.*, p. 270.
20. Section 2517.
21. Robinson, *op. cit.*, p. 270.
22. Reg. 20.2042-1(c)(2)-(6)
23. *Eleanor M. Schwager,* 64 T.C. 75 (1975).
24. Rev. Rul. 69-54, 1969-1 C.B. 221 and 72-307, 1972-1 C.B. 307.
25. Rev. Rul. 76-421, 1976-2, C.B. 300.
26. Rev. Rul. 76-490, 1976-2 C.B. 300.
27. *Estate of Bahen,* 305 F.2d 827, 62-2 USTC 12091 (1962).
28. Rev. Rul. 76-304, 1976-2 C.B. 269.
29. *Estate of Bogley,* 514 F.2d 1027, 75-1 USTC 13068 (Ct. Cls. 1975).
30. *Estate of Fried,* 54 T.C. 78 (1970).
31. *Estate of Porter,* 54 T.C. 103 (1970).
32. Nell Margulis, "Death-Benefit-Only Plans Create Estate Planning Opportunities for High-Tax-Bracket Executives," *Estate Planning* (July 1977), p. 284.

Appendix A
Inventory of Assets[*]

How to Use
These Schedules

THE primary purpose of this booklet is to assist you in developing, in permanent form, an inventory of assets for estate purposes. This record, along with supporting documents, should provide the executor of your estate with the data necessary to furnish tax basis information to your heirs, as now required by law.

To retain their usefulness, these schedules should be updated periodically. Each update should include:

Addition of assets acquired since the last update.

Addition of costs incurred for improvements.

Elimination of assets no longer owned.

This booklet, which may also be useful for insurance and estate planning purposes, should be kept with other important documents. The schedules and the footnotes that accompany them are designed to reflect the law in effect at January 1, 1977.

[*] These schedules are reprinted with permission from a booklet entitled "Inventory of Assets," © 1977 by Arthur Young & Company.

215

Footnotes

The schedules and footnotes in this booklet are designed to reflect the law in effect at January 1, 1977. [These numbers correspond to numbers found at the heads of columns on the following pages.]

(1) If actual date cannot be determined, list approximate date.
(2) If actual cost cannot be determined, indicate fair market value at date of acquisition.
(3) For property acquired by gift before December 31, 1976, indicate the amount of the donor's basis increased by the amount of Federal gift tax paid with respect to the gift. For property acquired by inheritance before December 31, 1976, indicate the value at which such property was included in the decedent's estate tax return. To determine the tax basis of other property not acquired by purchase, please consult your tax adviser.
(4) Enter total depreciation deducted in periods prior to January 1, 1977, if any.
(5) For property other than marketable bonds and securities, fair market value at December 31, 1976 need not be known in order to compute the tax basis of property acquired from a decedent. However, this information may be of value for estate and gift planning purposes.

The schedules begin on the next page.

MARKETABLE BONDS AND SECURITIES

FOR WHICH THERE IS A MARKET ON A STOCK EXCHANGE, AN OVER-THE-COUNTER MARKET, OR OTHERWISE

PROPERTY DESCRIPTION	OWNERSHIP INFORMATION			FINANCIAL INFORMATION		
	Date of acquisition (1)	How acquired? (purchase, gift, inheritance, etc.)	Ownership status: Community–C Joint–J Separate–S (Check all that apply)	For property owned jointly by husband and wife, indicate amounts provided by each	Total cost of property purchased (2)	Tax basis of property not acquired by purchase (3)	Market value at Dec. 31, 1976
			C J S		$	$	$
			C J S		$	$	$
			C J S		$	$	$
			C J S		$	$	$
			C J S		$	$	$
			C J S		$	$	$

OTHER BONDS AND SECURITIES

FOR WHICH THERE IS NO MARKET ON A STOCK EXCHANGE, AN OVER-THE-COUNTER MARKET, OR OTHERWISE

PROPERTY DESCRIPTION	OWNERSHIP INFORMATION			FINANCIAL INFORMATION		
	Date of acquisition (1)	How acquired? (purchase, gift, inheritance, etc.)	Ownership status: Community–C Joint–J Separate–S (Check all that apply)	For property owned jointly by husband and wife, indicate amounts provided by each	Total cost of property purchased (2)	Tax basis of property not acquired by purchase (3)	Approximate market value at Dec. 31, 1976 (5)
			C J S		$	$	$
			C J S		$	$	$
			C J S		$	$	$
			C J S		$	$	$
			C J S		$	$	$
			C J S		$	$	$

REAL ESTATE

OWNERSHIP INFORMATION

FINANCIAL INFORMATION

PROPERTY DESCRIPTION	Date of acquisition (1)	How acquired? (purchase, gift, inheritance, etc.)	Ownership status: Community—C Joint—J Separate—S (Check all that apply)	For property owned jointly by husband and wife, indicate amounts provided by each	Total cost of property purchased (Including cost of improvements) (2)	Tax basis of property not acquired by purchase (Including cost of improvements) (3)	Depreciation, amortization, or depletion prior to Jan. 1, 1977 (4)	Approximate market value at Dec. 31, 1976 (5)
			C J S		$	$	$	$
			C J S		$	$	$	$
			C J S		$	$	$	$
			C J S		$	$	$	$
			C J S		$	$	$	$
			C J S		$	$	$	$

PROPERTY OTHER THAN BONDS, SECURITIES, OR REAL ESTATE

OWNERSHIP INFORMATION

FINANCIAL INFORMATION

PROPERTY DESCRIPTION	Date of acquisition (1)	How acquired? (purchase, gift, inheritance, etc.)	Ownership status: Community–C Joint–J Separate–S (Check all that apply)	For property owned jointly by husband and wife, indicate amounts provided by each	Total cost of property purchased (including cost of improvements) (2)	Tax basis of property not acquired by purchase (including cost of improvements) (3)	Depreciation, amortization, or depletion prior to Jan. 1, 1977 (4)	Approximate market value at Dec. 31, 1976 (5)
			C J S		$	$	$	$
			C J S		$	$	$	$
			C J S		$	$	$	$
			C J S		$	$	$	$
			C J S		$	$	$	$
			C J S		$	$	$	$

Appendix B
Transfer Tax Rates

THE following table is taken from the *Instructions for Form 706, United States Estate Tax Return* (revised as of June 1977). The complete instruction booklet may be obtained from the Department of the Treasury, Internal Revenue Service.

Unified Rate Schedule

Column A	Column B	Column C	Column D
Taxable amount over	Taxable amount not over	Tax on amount in column A	Rate of tax on excess over amount in column A
			(Percent)
0	$10,000	0	18
$10,000	20,000	$1,800	20
20,000	40,000	3,800	22
40,000	60,000	8,200	24
60,000	80,000	13,000	26
80,000	100,000	18,200	28
100,000	150,000	23,800	30
150,000	250,000	38,800	32
250,000	500,000	70,800	34
500,000	750,000	155,800	37
750,000	1,000,000	248,300	39
1,000,000	1,250,000	345,800	41
1,250,000	1,500,000	448,300	43
1,500,000	2,000,000	555,800	45
2,000,000	2,500,000	780,800	49
2,500,000	3,000,000	1,025,800	53
3,000,000	3,500,000	1,290,800	57
3,500,000	4,000,000	1,575,800	61
4,000,000	4,500,000	1,880,800	65
4,500,000	5,000,000	2,205,800	69
5,000,000	----------------	2,550,800	70

Index

accountant, in estate planning, 19

adjusted gross estate (AGE): defined, 87–88; marital deduction, 76; tax installment provisions, 85

adjusted gross income to beneficiary, 133, 138–140

administration expenses, 57

allowable deductions, 56–59

alternative valuation, 47–49

American Law Institute, 128, 143

American Numismatic Association, 171

American Philatelic Society, 171

American Red Cross, 171

amount limitation on redeemed stock included in estate, 89–90

annuity: deferment of payments, qualified retirement plan, 196; in estate plan, 15; estate tax on, 192–193; fair market value, 47; in gross estate, 29–30; income tax on distribution, 186–187; rollover withdrawals, 198–199; selection of disbursement, 199

Arthur Young & Co., 3

assets: inventory of, 73, 215–220; miscellaneous, in gross estate, 36–39

apocalypse trust, 158–159

appointment powers, 164–166

appreciated capital gain property, 178–179

attorney, in estate planning, 18–19

layering, 161; lifetime,
15–17, 122–124; and marital
deduction, 61–62; to
minors, 110–112; of non-
qualified stock option, 203;
to private foundations,
177–178; requirements of,
96–98
gifts in contemplation of
death, gift tax on, 115–118
gift splitting, gift tax and,
100–102
gift tax, 95–96; computing,
113–124; deduction for
charitable gifts, 105–108;
exemptions, exclusions, and
unified credits, 99–113; on
gifts in contemplation of
death, 115–118; gift splitting and, 100–102; on in-
complete gifts, 115; marital
deduction and, 103–105;
parties subject to, 98–99;
present vs. future interest,
109–113; on revocable
transfers, 120–122; timing
of, 98–99; on transfers taking effect at death, 119–120;
on transfers with retained
life interest, 118–119
gift tax paid, in computation of
estate tax, 71–72
gift transfers, valuation of,
112–113
Girl Scouts of America, 171
grandchildren, generation-
skipping transfers to, 76–77
grandfather trusts, 146
Gregory case, 112
gross estate, 23–24; allowable

deductions, 57–59; alternate
valuation, 47–49; annuities
in, 29–30; computation of
tax, 67–72; dower or curtesy
interest, 24–25; fair market
value in, 42–47; gifts in,
34–36; inclusion of re-
deemed stock in, 87–89; life
insurance in, 31–32; marital
deductions, 59–67; power of
appointment in, 30–31;
property transfers in, 26–28;
real property interests in,
32–34; reduction by sys-
tematic lifetime giving, 73;
retained life interest in,
25–26; special-use valua-
tion, 49–51; tax, 68; tax basis
to beneficiaries, 51–55
Gutchess, A. D., 26

incidents of ownership, life
insurance, 204–205
income splitting and marital
deduction, 62–63
income tax: on annuity distribution, 186–187; death-
benefit-only plan, 190–191;
on life insurance benefits,
189–190; on profit-sharing
plans, 187–188; on retirement plans, 184–186; on
stock distributions, 188–189
incomplete gifts, gift tax on,
115
installment provision, estate
tax, 84–85
insurance, fair market value,
47
insurance policies, giving up